NIGHT PEOPLE

How To Be A DJ In '90s New York City

MARK RONSON

GRAND
CENTRAL

NEW YORK BOSTON

Copyright © 2025 by Mark Ronson
Cover design by Rodrigo Corral Studio
Cover copyright © 2025 by Hachette Book Group, Inc.

Grand Central Publishing
Hachette Book Group
1290 Avenue of the Americas, New York, NY 10104
grandcentralpublishing.com
@grandcentralpub

First Hardcover Edition: September 2025

Grand Central Publishing is a division of Hachette Book Group, Inc. The Grand Central Publishing name and logo is a registered trademark of Hachette Book Group, Inc.

The publisher is not responsible for websites (or their content) that are not owned by the publisher.

The Hachette Speakers Bureau provides a wide range of authors for speaking events. To find out more, go to hachettespeakersbureau.com or email HachetteSpeakers@hbgusa.com.

Grand Central Publishing books may be purchased in bulk for business, educational, or promotional use. For information, please contact your local bookseller or the Hachette Book Group Special Markets Department at special.markets@hbgusa.com.

Additional credits can be found on page 241.

Library of Congress Cataloging-in-Publication Data
Names: Ronson, Mark, 1975–author.
Title: Night people : how to be a DJ in '90s NYC / Mark Ronson.
Description: First hardcover edition. | New York : Grand Central Publishing, 2025. |
Identifiers: LCCN 2025013473 | ISBN 9781538741115 (hardcover) | ISBN 9781538741139 (ebook)
Subjects: LCSH: Ronson, Mark, 1975- | Disc Jockeys—New York (State)—New York—Biography. | Popular music—New York (State)—New York—1991–2000. | LCGFT: Autobiographies.
Classification: LCC ML429.R666 A3 2025 | DDC 782.42164/1554 [B]—dc23/eng/20250506
LC record available at https://lccn.loc.gov/2025013473

ISBNs: 978-1-5387-4111-5 (hardcover); 978-1-5387-7866-1 (hardcover, signed edition); 978-1-5387-4113-9 (ebook)

Printed in the United States of America

LSC-C

Printing 1, 2025

To Blu Jemz, a prince among Night People
and DJ AM, the most ferociously talented to step
behind club Technics

I'd never take "DJ" off "Clark Kent." It's because I'm a DJ that I've been able to do everything else I've done.

DJ CLARK KENT

People stomped inside the night
Let me climb into the night
Let me climb

MOS DEF, "CLIMB"

INTRODUCTION

The night is on your mind
Ayo the sun'll still shine
But now the night is on the mind

A TRIBE CALLED QUEST,
"MIDNIGHT" (1993)

2:00 A.M. You're at a house party packed with people rolling up from the club, all trying to squeeze a few more hours out of Saturday night. It's not wild, but it could get there. In the kitchen, bodies huddle around a counter, mixing bottom-shelf vodka with whatever's in reach—Capri-Sun, kombucha, maybe both. Out on the terrace, the diehards are smoking cigarettes like it's still 1999, ashing into a cereal bowl that's been sacrificed for the occasion.

In the living room, speakers pump out a mishmash of bedroom-pop and the occasional boy-band classic. Somebody's go-to playlist. It's ironic, tolerable—and ultimately a bit lifeless. *You* can feel it, though: The party is on the verge. It just needs someone brave enough to tip it over.

You pull out your phone and cue up your surefire banger. Sliding over to the speaker, you hijack the aux cord like it's nothing, and—

"ZZZZZZRRT! KRRRKKKK!!!"

A sharp electronic buzz rips through the room.

Eyes snap toward you. The judgment is heavy.

But then your fingertip makes contact and the opening kick drums of Fatman Scoop's "Be Faithful" tear through the room like blows from Thor's hammer. The shift is seismic. Cups slam to countertops, the sofa gets shoved back, bodies flood the floor with raised hands—a collective *FINALLY* overtakes the place. You stand by the speaker, cradling your phone like a trophy. The room is alive, buzzing, and, somehow, united. Your finger hovers over the screen to cue up the next heater. The crowd now trusts you. You're about to show them why.

* * *

Now you're in the club. The DJ is holding it down steady; the blends are clean if predictable. A seven out of ten. But you're with your crew, and you know the one song that would spark a pretty pandemonium.

You make your move, weaving through the crowd, navigating sloshed drinks, wobbly heels, and an elbow to the ribs, until you're at the booth. You tap the DJ on the shoulder. She turns, her face equal parts curiosity and dread. (No DJ is ever pumped to see a rando approaching.)

"Yeah?" she says.

"Hey, it's my friend's birthday, and we were wondering if you could play 'My Neck, My Back,' by Khia."

It's a lie, of course. But a harmless one. The DJ exhales, visibly relieved you're not the fifth person to request "Don't Stop Believin'."

"Got you," she says, fingers already flying across the laptop, cueing it up.

You head back to your table, anticipation building. And then, two tracks later, the opening bars hit:

"All you ladies, pop yo'…like this…" The first 808 snare drum pierces the air. The whole place knows Khia's filthy sing-along better than their own Social Security numbers. From the windows to the wall, around every banquette and booth, everyone is up on their feet. By the time the beat drops and the hook lands, the walls shake like they might come down. You're in the center of it all, hands on knees, and catch your breath for a moment, just to take it all in. More than a request, this was a gift to your crew and the other hundred people up in here. As well as the DJ, who shoots you a look of appreciation. You stand there drunk on power—and Grey Goose.

But mostly power.

The first time you feel this sensation, nothing compares. You think to yourself, This isn't like sex; it's like sex with three hundred people at once. A high fueled by our strongest instincts: connection, belonging, sharing, and compassion. Yes, compassion. Don't laugh—you're giving the room a feeling they didn't even know they needed when they stepped out their doors. The joy is reciprocal, passing back and forth like an endless feedback loop of human happiness. Or some shit like that. (It's hard to articulate. You're a little tipsy.)

And then there's the control.

Oh, how I *loved* that control.

For someone who grew up amid chaos and uncertainty, the DJ booth was the perfect refuge—a one-man command center, where every fader and dial bent the world to my will.

Validation, belonging? My years as a DJ in New York's nineties club scene blessed me with an abundance of both.

And then there was the music itself: Gang Starr, A Tribe Called Quest, the Meters, Public Enemy, Stevie Wonder. My great obsession.

At seventeen, I knew I'd never be able to rhyme like Q-Tip or bang out beats as raw as Pete Rock's. But I could play their music and shape something out of my devotion using two Technics 1200s and a mixer. Those tools were my first love, and this is a story about that love—the thing that's informed everything I've done since. It's a tale of nineties New York—a time when DJing wasn't about being a Spotify lord, punching play on your biggest tunes in Vegas for two hundred stacks. Rather, it was the domain of faceless maestros who knew a disco classic like Players Association's "Turn the Music Up!" as well as they knew Junior M.A.F.I.A.'s "Player's Anthem," and we played both in the Lower East Side for one hundred and fifty dollars per night. Alongside my fellow DJs, I worked batshit hours, dealt with lunatic club owners, and carted hundreds of pounds of vinyl up five flights of stairs four times a week in order to spend most nights in a tiny booth, all alone. My eardrums emerged battered, and there were other costs, too. But it was all worth it—for that feeling.

I was ten years old when I got my first hit of it.

* * *

In 1985, after several years together, my mother, Ann, and step-father, Mick, decided to get married. They threw a low-key wedding in the garden of a summer rental. Pale balloons from the local party store bobbed gently around tables draped in white cloth. That, along with the chuppah, was the entirety of the décor.

INTRODUCTION

My mother delighted in any chance to upend social norms and spent her final moments as an unmarried woman parading my cherubic one-year-old brother, Alexander, around to the guests, asking, "Anyone want to hold him in his last few minutes as a bastard?"

There was no band, no DJ. Even though my stepfather, Mick Jones, was the lead guitarist in the rock group Foreigner, the music at his own wedding seemed an afterthought. Some preloaded tapes—Chuck Berry, Buddy Holly—played through a couple of large speakers in the garden, connected to a cassette deck tucked inside the house. And then, as the sun began to set, the music stopped entirely.

Mick turned to me. "Mark, go put something on." This was the most profound responsibility that I could have been given. I was obsessed with audio equipment. My happiest times with Mick were in his home studio, surrounded by the warmth of tape machines and synthesizers and the soft yellow-green glow of digital meters. I'd sit quietly for hours as he recorded demos, watching his hands turn dials and flip switches. Knobs and faders transformed the room into a place where anything wrong could be fixed, adjusted, or set right. When I was there, I was untouched by the worries and unease of the outside world.

When Mick handed me this task, I felt the fate of the party in my hands. I bolted into the house, skidding into the living room, where a messy pile of cassettes lay scattered on the floor. I dove into them, tossing aside Taj Mahal and Robert Cray. Too bluesy. Too niche. I needed something universal, something perfect.

Time Pieces: The Best of Eric Clapton. A-ha. I flipped it over, scanned the track list, and there it was: "Wonderful Tonight." My mother loved that song. Even at ten, I knew the lyrics were a fit.

INTRODUCTION

I jammed the cassette into the player, hit auto-cue to find track four on side A, and pressed play. The first notes of Clapton's guitar drifted from the speakers, the sound melting into the warm night air. I felt the rush of knowing *I'd* chosen this song. I peered through the big bay windows. My memory here is blurry, but in my mind, Mick reached for my mother. She looked almost luminescent, her white dress glowing under the rising moon. He pulled her into a slow dance as Clapton bent the notes to make his guitar sing.

For the first time in my life, I knew I'd done something right.

ONE

I AM A NIGHT PERSON, just like my parents before me.

My mother, Ann, grew up in a large Jewish family, one of five children. Her mother, Judith, died of cancer when my mother was eleven. Her father, Fred, was a "doctor of medicine"—what we'd now call an internist—who fled his home of Austria in 1937, barely escaping the Nazis, and made a new life in England.

After his wife's death, Fred was driven by a restless desire to move, and frequently uprooted the family on a whim. He would spin a globe and take them wherever his finger landed: Liverpool, Auckland, Perth, back to Liverpool, then Australia again, London, and back to New Zealand. Like he was always searching for Judith.

Fred worked tirelessly to provide for his children. They weren't wealthy, but they never lacked nice clothes, shoes, or fresh fruit. Though my mother had an older brother, much of the responsibility for caring for three younger siblings fell on her. Moving to so many new cities, always being the new "Jew girl," posed constant challenges. She found solace in the night, painting and writing poetry in the quiet hours after the house fell silent. But like her father, she had a restless spirit. At twenty, she left school and her father's Liverpool home, feeling the pull of London.

My father, Laurence, grew up in a small, affluent Jewish family in North London. His father, Henry, came from hard-nosed East End stock—a former heavyweight boxer in the Jewish Lads' Brigade who spent his youth brawling with fascists in the streets of East London. Over time, he built a family furniture business from nothing and, with the help of his astute eldest son Gerald—who was ten years older than my father—transformed it into one of Britain's largest property companies, Heron.

My father's path was laid out before he could tie his laces. He was expected to enter Heron at the bottom rung and follow in Gerald's footsteps. There was never any debate about these matters in the Ronson household. The family practiced tough love, talking about "the Ronson Temper" as if it were a curse carried with them from Russia in the 1800s.

My grandmother Sarah had a record player in the study that my father liked to play with, and once he got his hands on a 45 of "Fingertips," by Little Stevie Wonder, he was sprung. Every Friday, he hurried to One Stop Records on South Molton Street to scroll through the new R&B imports from the States. He became obsessed with the raw sound of Booker T. & the M.G.'s and Otis Redding. When he got older, he broke from the family business to make his way in the music industry. He grew his hair long—an unmistakable "fuck you"—and leaned into the things he loved: fast cars, loud music, and raising a bit of hell.

My parents met at a wedding in 1974. My mother had been

invited there by a boy who, she had recently discovered, had a girl-friend. Annoyed, she went anyway—mainly to spite him. She wore a tight black velvet dress with one of the Seven Dwarfs stitched on the back, sure that it would embarrass him at a bourgeois Hampstead wedding. My father spotted her from across the room—he knew a fellow rebel when he saw one. A few days later, he called to ask her out. She teased him: "Sorry, I don't date poor little rich boys." He fell madly in love, she followed suit, and they were married within a year. I made my debut nine months later. Two years after that, my twin sisters, Charlotte and Samantha, arrived.

My parents were young and rich, and lived for the party. My father founded a music publishing company and discovered the writer of Bucks Fizz's Eurovision-winning smash "Making Your Mind Up," among others. His circle was filled with rock stars, and their unofficial headquarters was Tramp—the most glamorous nightclub in 1970s London. Tramp was packed with musicians, actors, and the occasional royal. Many of them spilled back to our house on Circus Road—a fitting name for a place overrun by party animals, rock stars, and Keith Moon, the patron saint of both. My mother loved playing hostess. She told me, "Why would I go to someone else's and have to stumble home hungover?"

My earliest memories are all tied to the night. The first, when I was three, begins with my bedroom door cracking open. I sat up in my captain's bed as my mother walked in, followed by Robin Williams—or rather, as I knew him, Mork from *Mork & Mindy*. Why my favorite TV character was suddenly standing over my bed, I didn't know, but it didn't feel unusual.

Robin and my mother emitted a zany energy, but I was used to how adults behaved at night. They were always more fun and less irritable. Shouting, tension—those were for the day.

Robin kept peeking through the curtains, like someone was watching from the street. "Robin," my mother said, laughing, "it's St John's Wood, not the Kremlin. There are no spies down there." She coaxed him away from the window and he came over, tucked me into my truck-patterned sheets, and went to leave.

"Mork," I called out after him. "You forgot…"

"Nanu Nanu," he said with a smile, delivering his signature catchphrase.

"Nanu Nanu," I echoed, drifting back to sleep.

Other nights, the strains of seventies funk—the Bar-Kays, the Commodores, and Parliament—stirred me awake, calling from down the hall. I'd wander into the living room, a mop-topped munchkin weaving between grown-ups, dodging lit cigarettes, drawn to the source of the sound. My mother wasn't bothered if we woke up at odd hours—she liked to show us off, as long as we got back into bed after a few laps around the party. I loved standing so close to the stereo I could feel the scratchy speaker fabric against my face as I crossed my right hand over my left to mimic what the drummer was playing.

Our house was fine as long as it was night and the stereo was blasting. Otherwise, funky drummers were replaced by fiercely slammed doors. Instead of the badass bass of Graham Central Station, an opera of angry crescendos and heavy silences played from behind my parents' bedroom door.

I don't have many memories from zero to five—who does? But I remember the feeling: anxiety, uncertainty, and negative anticipation, the ground constantly shifting under me while I was too young to piece together the logic of what was happening. There was a fear that never quite left, and a constant watchfulness that became instinct before I understood why. During the day, a stifling tension hung in the air. In pictures from that time, I'm either blank-faced or mugging for the camera, tap-dancing to distract or cheer someone up. I got good at walking on eggshells, but inevitably, one would crack. My mother and father were good people, but not good together.

My parents separated when I was five, and things soon got better for everyone. A year later, a guy named Mick showed up at the door to take my mother on a date. He was from Somerset, a rural county near Stonehenge in southwest England. He now lived in New York but happened to be passing through London for a few days. My mother told me he played in a band, and he patiently answered my many questions about what a "lead guitarist" did—and whether he'd ever been on the Muppets—while she got dressed upstairs.

It didn't take long for them to fall in love. Soon my mother, my two sisters, and I moved from London to New York with him, squeezing into his bachelor pad on Riverside Drive. Mick's band, Foreigner, was an arena giant thanks to a string of hits like "Cold as Ice," "Hot Blooded," and "Juke Box Hero." He soon wrote the future gospel-rock anthem "I Want to Know What Love Is" for my mother. He tried to convince her that the ballad "Waiting for a Girl Like You" was also written for her—even though it came out before they met. She wasn't falling for the psychic songwriting pitch, but she appreciated that he was a romantic.

They moved into a ten-room apartment on Central Park West that my mother turned into a neon-rococo-glam-rock fantasy in which pink cherub candelabras, Persian rugs, French deco cabinets, and a 1950s Wurlitzer jukebox coexisted in chaotic harmony. I kept my habit of waking up in the middle of the night, stumbling into after-parties teeming with musicians and eccentrics who were always buzzy and keen to know how I was doing and what music I liked.

Andy Warhol even made a surprise appearance. A riveting entry from *The Andy Warhol Diaries*, Thursday, January 9, 1986: "Left at 5:00 to go uptown to...[a] party at Ann Ronson's....There was no food. Just three pieces of chicken sushi. I found some caviar on a tray in the corner of a room where you would never look." (If Andy had checked the freezer, he'd have found enough casseroles to feed the entire Factory for a month—my mother was big on preparing meals in bulk, a habit left over from a childhood of cooking for five siblings.)

Even better were the nights when I discovered Mick sitting up alone in his home studio listening to mixes for the next Foreigner album. I was fascinated why there were eight versions of the same song: one where the bass was softer, another with the lead vocal louder, one with less reverb. He'd play them for me, and I'd tell him which one I liked best. He liked my input enough to start waking me at 3:00 a.m. on school nights to get my feedback—letting a sleepy sixth grader help shape the sound of rock radio.

Music consumed me. I started guitar and saxophone lessons and pored over Mick's weekly copy of *Billboard*, a music industry bible of charts and gossip that arrived every Friday. Mick let me use his home studio, where I spent hours at his Synclavier—a state-of-the-art, two-hundred-thousand-dollar digital synthesizer capable of programming and recording entire songs. I once sat for two days meticulously remaking "Wishing Well" by Terence Trent D'Arby, starting with the drumbeat, then layering the bass line, the chords, and finally adding the whistling melody on top. I loved deconstructing the song to understand its magic, as much as the solitude and sense of control that the studio provided.

Every holiday, my sisters and I flew back to London to spend time with my father, who also became more fun after the split. Looking like seventies Al Pacino through an Ashkenazi filter, he chain-smoked Rothmans and gunned noisy sports cars way too fast through quaint London streets, blasting Little Feat and Prince. Strangers stopped to ask him if he was a rock star more frequently than they did Mick. His ear for talent still sharp, he discovered a young musician named Andrew Roachford, whose soulful voice and songwriting caught his attention. He began managing Roachford and got him signed to Columbia Records; his debut single, "Cuddly Toy," went Top 5 in the UK.

My father was inappropriate in the best way. He taught us fantastic swear words and intentionally misinformed us of their meanings. After dinner one night Samantha, age five, leaned back in her chair, let out a contented sigh, and exclaimed, "Bollocks!"

"WHAT DID YOU SAY?!" my mother yelled.

"I said, 'Bollocks!'" she said, thoroughly confused. "I thought that's what you say after a good meal."

Another time, while doing the crossword on the side of a McDonald's Happy Meal, I asked my father for a five-letter word for something that goes in a Big Mac. "Vomit," he replied. I filled in the squares and held on to this mistruth for years.

At twelve, I spent the first part of the summer interning at *Rolling Stone*, making coffee, tallying album charts, and routing incoming calls through the high-tech PBX switchboard. During breaks, I quietly memorized my Bar Mitzvah haftorah portion. For the rest of that summer, I led a music class at a Jewish day camp. I didn't know any children's songs, so I tweaked the lyrics to the songs I did know. Bad Company's "Feel Like Makin' Love" became Camp Karole's "Feel Like Makin' Lunch." I attended the prestigious Collegiate School for Boys, where I got teased for my hybrid accent. Half the class called me "Commie"—in 1984, people were fired up about the Cold War, even though I came from England, not Estonia. I made a close friend named Sean, who lived two blocks away from me, in the Dakota, and went to another school. My odd, prepubescent mid-Atlantic alto confounded his doorman each time I visited.

"Hello, can you please tell Sean that Mark is here?"

"Maarg?"

"No. Marrrck," I said, trying to sound more American.

"Merck?"

"No, sorry, it's Mahhk." Back to British.

"Mog?"

"Sure."

This went on for months until I finally changed my name to "Mog." At least when visiting Sean's lobby. When I returned to London for school holidays, my old friends teased me for sounding like a "Yank, already." I felt that I was no longer a Brit and not really an American. Barely twelve, I knew I'd never fully fit in anywhere.

Sean's best friend, Max—the son of restaurant magnate Warner LeRoy—lived below him, in a duplex apartment adorned with Frank Stella sculptures and Kandinsky paintings. His bedroom had twelve-foot ceilings, thick royal-blue carpet, and—most important—a drum kit and a Marshall amp. We spent our after-school hours terrorizing his parents with balls to the wall attempts at Living Colour's "Cult of Personality" and Hendrix's "Stone Free." Max was the most magnetic kid imaginable—bursting with warmth. He could also be gloriously impulsive. In ninth grade, with his parents out of town, he threw a house party that spiraled into chaos and their place got trashed. Facing a severe grounding, he offered me up as the mastermind.

Sean's mother was Yoko Ono; his father was John Lennon, who had been cruelly taken from him several years before we met—a profound tragedy for anyone, let alone a child. Even at twelve, he exhibited his father's sharp wit and charisma. The Dakota apartment was always full of fascinating characters. During the *Bad* tour, Michael Jackson stayed over. Michael just wanted to goof around and toss "soggies"—tightly packed mounds of wet toilet paper—out the window. Meanwhile, I was fixated on getting a hit song out of him to take back to Mick's home studio.

"Michael, Michael, stand still for a sec and sing us a bass line!" I pleaded.

Finally, to shut me up, he hummed something loosely regurgitated from "Smooth Criminal" and went back to sprinting up and down the long hallway and shining his laser pointer out the window.

He seemed like more of a kid than we did. I'm still not sure what was stranger: hanging out with Michael Jackson and throwing soaked Charmin balls onto the street or that it felt normal. I never told anyone at school—even then, I understood how ridiculous it would be to name-drop at that level. (Clearly, my sense of decorum has eroded.)

Another time, Keith Haring, who was friends with Yoko, smuggled us into Area, a nightclub not unlike the ones I'd later lose myself in—pitch dark, too much fun, with nowhere comfortable to sit. I had a sense we weren't supposed to be there, which made it even better.

* * *

The summer I turned fourteen, Sean called to tell me he and Max were heading off to a fancy boarding school in Europe. "We'll still have the summers to jam," he said brightly, but I was overcome with a sadness I'd never known. I hung up the phone and slunk to the floor, feeling my first heartbreak. I soon formed a new band, though—a bunch of city kids with one of the worst band names you've ever heard. The only advantage to calling ourselves "The Whole Earth Mamas" was that we got booked at several feminist rallies. Puzzled looks greeted us as we took the stage. ("Hey, those kids aren't, er, Mamas.") We shuffled some players around, practiced a lot, and even got close to sounding like our heroes, the funk-metal virtuosos 24-7 Spyz and Living Colour.

Mike Pollard, our lead guitarist, had twisted braids that whipped around like the blades of a chopper when shredding his Ibanez. Billy Chang was sixteen and could slap and pop like Jaco Pastorius. He had dreads, too, and a scruffy goatee, the kind grown to declare your manhood but that only gets you carded quicker. Scott Smith, our ace drummer, begrudgingly played our funk rock while dreaming of Morrissey. And Sean Zanni, our lead singer, had the soulful, scratchy voice of someone who'd been smoking Marlboro Reds since the age of twelve—because he had.

In fact, everyone was so good, the widening chasm between my abilities and theirs was becoming hard to ignore. They were shredders, and I was solid. Maybe a solid plus. I had discipline and drive, just not the kind that chained you to a chair for six hours straight, running the Aeolian scale ad nauseam. The previous summer, I'd gone to a guitar camp in Massachusetts, hoping it would boost my technical abilities. Instead, it became another reminder that most guitarists my age were flat-out more gifted than me. Sean Lennon and I had always been at roughly the same level—or so I thought. Then he came back from a holiday in Brazil playing like Antônio Carlos Jobim. If *that's* what being a guitarist sounds like, I thought, I need to find a new thing.

During the obligatory solo sections of our gigs, I hoped someone might pull the fire alarm before my turn, sparing both me and the crowd. Still, I loved the behind-the-scenes work—engineering and recording our demos, designing and handing out flyers, raiding my mother's closet for ridiculous stage clothes, and scoring gigs. So I kept at it.

I spotted an ad in *The Village Voice*: Giant Step, a popular soul and jazz party, was taking over Sweet Jane's for the New Music Seminar—a weeklong showcase of cutting-edge bands. I'd already snuck into a few of their parties to catch my favorite band, the Brand New Heavies, which is how I first met Maurice Bernstein, Giant Step's founder. A Manchester transplant, Maurice had landed in

New York in the late eighties with empty pockets and blagged his way into a job at a fancy Italian restaurant by passing himself off as a former headwaiter at Claridge's, London's most prestigious hotel. After cycling through a few more restaurant gigs, he cofounded Giant Step—which became one of the city's hippest nights out.

At the next Giant Step party, I made a beeline for him.

"I saw the ad for Sweet Jane's. You should put my band on the bill!"

"What's your band called again? Mother Earth's Garden Bistro?" Maurice asked genuinely. "Sorry, the bill's full."

Desperation kicked in. "What if my friend Sean got up with us?" I blurted, startled by my own guile.

"Sean who?" he asked.

"Sean Lennon," I replied, a sticky sweat now breaking across my skin.

"If you do that, I'll put you on."

The good news was I'd scored us our biggest gig ever. The bad news was I'd sold out my best friend to do it. Sean was home for the summer, so I headed to the Dakota to pitch him the idea.

"I got the band an amazing gig at the New Music Seminar. It'd be so cool if you got up and played a song with us," I said, skipping over most of the story.

He mulled it over. Sean thought the world of me but not so much the band I'd thrown myself into while he was away. "I guess we could play 'Release,'" he said, referring to the brooding closer from Pearl Jam's *Ten*—an album we listened to incessantly. "Max'll play guitar and I'll sing." I knew a nine-minute grunge opus was hardly what the jazzy Giant Step crowd came for, but I was just relieved to have Sean on board.

On gig day, we showed up to sound check, but there was no sign of Sean or Max, and I began to panic. I called their homes, no answer. I paged Sean "911" and waited anxiously by the pay phone in Sweet Jane's. When he finally called back, he explained that he and Max had dropped acid an hour ago and wandered off to Central Park. He didn't want to play the gig. My heart sank into my Doc Martens.

"Sean, I really need you to play tonight. It's a big deal for us and now they're expecting you, too," I said, my baggy pants practically on fire.

"Yeah, it just feels weird," he said, picking up on something. "It's your band. Why are we doing this?"

I wanted to say, "Because I used your name to get the gig and I'm a bad friend." Instead, I hung up and bolted for a cab uptown.

* * *

Sheep Meadow, a vast fifteen-acre field at the southern end of Central Park, was the geographic and cultural center of our high school scene. Unlike the manicured lawns and kiddie carousels found in the rest of the park, the Meadow was its own universe. Hippies with matted hair sang "Redemption Song" so sincerely you *almost* forgave them. There were stoners in oversized oval sunglasses and silver peace sign pendants; "hard rocks" in baggy jeans and backpacks filled with Krylon graffiti markers planning their next boosting mission; and Catholic schoolgirls in gray flannel skirts, white socks, and penny loafers who sat in circles flashing teenage thigh. The Meadow wasn't just a patch of grass, it was our after-school meeting point, hang zone, and one-stop shop to score weed, acid, and overpriced

Snapple. Most days, I bounced between cliques with my CD boom box playing Mary's Danish, Jesus Jones, and Smashing Pumpkins. Or Main Source or LL Cool J. Depending on the crew. But today, I carried no boom box, just guilt and despair.

Luckily, the park was nearly empty but for the hardcore dropouts and dealers. I spotted Sean and Max right away. As I ran over, they were laid out on their backs staring up at the clouds watching a dragon eat a pizza, or two dolphins high-fiving, or whatever magical shit the LSD was serving them. My adrenaline was pumping so hard, I have no memory of what I said, but somehow I managed to bundle them both into Sean's kaftan, then herd them into a taxi and down to sound check.

* * *

Sweet Jane's—all concrete and peeling paint—was on the ground floor of a former boardinghouse for sailors. At the corner of Jane Street and the West Side Highway, it once housed the surviving passengers from the *Titanic* when they arrived in New York. The venue was packed the moment the doors opened, thanks to the headliners: the Boston rap group Ed O.G. and da Bulldogs, and Pal Joey—whose "Hot Music" was the jazz-house anthem of the Giant Step scene. We'd landed the hottest ticket in town, stepping onto the stage to a sea of Black and white hipsters in Kangols, Fred Perry jackets, and leather Afrocentric medallions.

As we tore into our first tune, it was clear our sound—overdriven guitars, crash cymbals, bluesy warbling—wasn't exactly the vibe. We received thirty seconds of polite curiosity followed by puzzled glances, and then total lack of interest. I kept my head down and powered through.

During our final song, Sean stood, radiating junior rock star bravado with his Les Paul slung low and long dark hair hanging straight down. But it was the rock 'n' roll epic no one had asked for. When it ended, I slunk offstage, avoiding all eye contact with the Giant Step cognoscenti.

Sean and Max slipped out before I could catch them. Left behind, I packed up my amp and waited to help Scott, our drummer, load out. I felt a trifecta of shame: the embarrassment of our shit performance, the knowledge that we'd only made the bill because of Sean, and the guilt of lying to him. This was supposed to be our best gig ever. Instead, it felt more like the last. Half the band was heading off to college next year. For the past two years, the group had been my identity and the focus of all my musical ambitions. What was I going to do without it? Sean was already playing circles around me. I could hole up in Mick's studio recording demo tracks, but what was the point? I couldn't rap or sing. Was it all over? The thought was too big to let in.

After an hour of gear *Tetris*, we'd crammed my bulky Roland Jazz Chorus amp and Scott's entire drum kit into the back of his stepfather's Mazda 626 and headed uptown. I looked forward to these late-night rides with Scott. His stoic soulfulness was calming. He doled out life advice on music and girls, wisdom you might absorb from an older brother or father—neither of which I had readily available. His own father died when he was young, and it seemed to have fast-tracked him to an understanding of grown-up matters.

As we cruised up Tenth Avenue with the summer night air blowing through the windows, I finally exhaled. On a good night, we'd dissect the highs, replay the best moments, and talk about how to improve our set. But tonight, there was nothing to say. We let the white noise of the West Side Highway fill the silence.

Scott loved Tenth Avenue, always repeating how, at night, you could catch every light all the way uptown. He said it like it was one of the few dependable things in his life. He punched play on the cassette deck, and the prelude of Pete Rock & C.L. Smooth's "They Reminisce over You (T.R.O.Y.)" filled the car. A rap song whose melancholy matched our own. I'd always been drawn to hip-hop for the furious breakbeats and defiant energy of Public Enemy or LL. But this was something else: haunting, understated, getting under my skin in a new way.

Scott made a left and pulled up outside his house. I loved how West Seventieth Street ran right up to the water's edge, as if Robert Moses had run out of asphalt. We stood for a moment, staring at the half-lit skyline of Jersey City. I asked if I could crash at his place. His too-small couch was preferable to the emptiness of my parents' apartment, with my sisters at camp and my mother and Mick on tour.

Later, sprawled across the couch and unable to sleep, I found myself pulled toward the stereo, needing to hear that cassette once more. The song's opening caught me off guard again: ten seconds of upbeat frantic northern soul that then dissolved into a mournful saxophone loop.

The sample wasn't quite jazz or funk—more like a warm, hippie soul. C.L. Smooth's half-rapped, half-spoken verses touched on all kinds of loss: innocence, friendships, the absence of a father, the evaporation of dreams. Pete Rock's lo-fi beat, with its perfectly programmed accents and rat-a-tat snare rolls, was a new kind of drumming.

As sad as the song was making me feel, I couldn't stop replaying it, chasing the ache. I wanted to live inside this song, its grit and melancholy.

Fuck my band. This was the future. I didn't care if I couldn't rap or make beats—I had to find my way into this world.

TWO

SIX MONTHS LATER, on a Wednesday night—a school night—
I stood frozen in panic beneath the thirty-foot vaulted ceilings
of a neo-Gothic chapel. It was fall of '92, senior year. I was at a club
called Limelight, which was housed in an enormous Episcopal
church on Sixth Avenue, at the eastern edge of Chelsea. The main
dance floor could hold three thousand kids, but I never spent much
time there. I was too busy tripping on acid and losing myself in
Limelight's labyrinth of chapels and chambers.

Wednesdays belonged to Disco 2000, which was masterminded
by a promoter named Michael Alig. Alig was one of the ringlead-
ers of a group of young nightlife figures who the media dubbed the
"Club Kids." They were both kids and walking art projects, covered
in ghoulish makeup and whatever outlandish fabrics or trash they
could stitch together. Most of them were oddly beautiful. They followed Alig around Limelight as if he was some kind of hedonistic
Pied Piper. I wasn't particularly edgy or weird looking, but Alig

wanted to fill his parties with a younger crowd, and so, on Wednesdays, the doors opened wider for revelers like me.

That night, my friends and I had snorted something called Special K. But twenty minutes later, they were nowhere to be found, and I couldn't move my legs. Just a few months ago, I'd never touched drugs. I was a good boy with both feet planted firmly on the ground. Now, my platform Pumas were glued to it.

The music seemed like it had suddenly turned cold, ricocheting off the brittle concrete. Strobes flashed too fast for me to see ahead, the sensory overload like a vise. I tried lifting one foot. Nothing. Using all my strength, I managed to raise one leg and replant it six inches in front of me. Step by tiny step, I stumbled out of the room and collapsed onto a bench by the toilets. My girlfriend, Kim, found me and sat down, holding my hand. A beautiful stained-glass depiction of Jesus gazed down from above.

I stared into his glowing purple aura and began a silent conversation.

Dear Jesus, if you make this horrible feeling go away, I promise never to party in your house again. So please deliver me from evil and into a taxi—preferably without having to walk too far up Sixth.

My oath lasted one week. Limelight was just too much fun. Growing up, I'd venture downtown to play shows at CBGB, Wetlands, and the Bitter End. But club culture was a different world. My stepbrother Roman told me stories of dancing onstage at the Palladium to De La Soul. It all sounded like something for cool older siblings. Suddenly, though, I found myself right in the middle of it, at the white-hot center of the flame.

Disco 2000 was candy-striped chaos: thousands of teens off their faces, most of them wearing some variation of what was the standard-issue rave uniform: T-shirts, giant JNCO jeans, and floppy bucket hats. Some of the girls were in ten-inch platform sneakers and knee-high socks, their hair held back with little pink barrettes. Most of Michael Alig's Club Kids gave the impression they'd devour your soul for breakfast, but I liked some of them, like Richie Rich—a disarmingly kind platinum blond with Weimar eyebrows. And Jenny Talia, who had a shaved head and wore black lipstick and piercings all over, was a sweetheart who played high school softball with Kim. More proof that night and day were separate universes.

Limelight oozed a depraved energy at times. Seedy old people (to us, anyone above the age of twenty) wandered the rooms looking to ply wayward youths with ketamine and Rohypnol. But overall, it was a three-story fun house that admitted us without any questions, so we weren't complaining.

Every week, I followed the same ritual. Wednesdays were devoted to Disco 2000. Thursdays belonged to the Stretch Armstrong and Bobbito radio show on WKCR—a four-hour odyssey of underground hip-hop. If Pete Rock & C.L. Smooth had been my gateway, then Stretch and Bobbito opened the floodgates. Lord Finesse, Diamond D, Das EFX, Black Moon, Showbiz & A.G.—the list was endless.

The show aired at 1:00 a.m., way past bedtime. So I'd pop in a Maxell XLII cassette, set my stereo to record, and collapse into bed, knowing I'd be waking up to two hours of gold. By morning, the tape was in my Sony Sports Walkman soundtracking my walk to school. More than a radio show, it was a new musical encyclopedia, a language. I listened to my tapes so much, I even knew the banter by heart, smiling quietly, finishing the DJs' jokes before they did.

I wanted to find a way into making the sort of music that I was suddenly devouring nonstop. One Friday in the school rec room my classmate Conrad Meertins, an aspiring emcee, walked by. "What's this track?" I asked, passing him the headphones.

"'DWYCK,' by Gang Starr," he said without hesitation. Then, casually, "By the way, me, Mike, and Jerry signed up for this talent show at Stuyvesant. Think you could make us a beat in your stepfather's studio?"

"Sure," I said, trying to contain my excitement.

"All right, I'm late for history. Peace."

After school, I made my daily pilgrimage to a record store on West Seventy-Second Street called HMV, a multistory music paradise. I spent hours there, running my fingers over every cassette, making sure I didn't miss a single title. This time, I went straight to the hip-hop section and asked for the most recent Gang Starr album.

I took it home, hit play, and was obliterated by the hard drums and hypnotic ride cymbal of "Place Where We Dwell." DJ Premier's beats were jazzy and soulful, with the force of a right hook to the gut. Guru's raps struck the same balance—intelligence, menace, romance all rolled into one. This was my new favorite album.

The next week, Conrad, Mike Lee Yow, and Jerry Bright came over to work on their track for the contest, to be judged by the Rev. Al Sharpton. They were the only three Black students in a class of fifty. Collegiate wasn't exactly a cradle of diversity. There were other kids who listened to rap. One of my best friends, Daniel Sauli—an Italian Jew with a bold Akira tattoo and an earring that clashed with the school's blazer-and-tie orthodoxy—loved Gang Starr and EPMD. The white kids who were on partial athletic scholarships, and commuted from downtown and Brooklyn, put me on to Eric B. & Rakim. But Conrad, Mike, and Jerry were the only emcees I knew.

I had no clue how to make a track for their rap talent show, and if I'd been a better friend, I might've admitted I'd never touched a sampler before. But I'd been listening to *Daily Operation* nonstop, obsessed with Premier's production style—funky samples layered with hard-hitting drums—and figured I could just try and mimic it.

Mick happened to have an Akai S950 digital sampler—Premier's weapon of choice—in his studio. After wrestling with its tiny LCD interface for an hour, I still couldn't sync a Meters drumbeat with a two-bar loop from "The Word," by the Beatles. I figured it was a wash until I spotted another keyboard with a built-in sampler. Loading one sample into each, I aligned the tempos and stood like the Phantom of the Opera, arms outstretched, punching both buttons every three seconds for five minutes straight.

Mike watched me as I worked. "What you're doing is a lot like DJing, matching beats and whatnot. I think you'd like it," he said.

He might as well have suggested I take up basket weaving. For all the hours I spent devouring Stretch and Bobbito, the thought of being a DJ had never crossed my mind.

"Cool," I answered, too busy sweating over keeping the beat on track to think much more about it.

A week later, I sat on the edge of my seat in the auditorium of Stuyvesant High School as our homemade beat blasted through the PA. The guys were a bit shy but held their own, and I liked our chances—until two thirteen-year-olds stormed the stage like squirrels on Ritalin, rapping over the instrumental to "Jump," by Kris Kross. The place went bananas, and I knew it was a wrap.

* * *

Wednesday was Disco 2000, Thursday was for Stretch and Bobbito, and Friday was the main event: NASA at the Shelter. The Shelter—at 157 Hudson Street in Tribeca—sprawled across half the block, its red-brick façade punctuated by enormous arched windows that looked out onto the cobblestone street below. Once a stable for American Express, the building had towering doors sized for horse-drawn wagons. These days, it housed a mad weekly rave where kids from across the boroughs, as young as thirteen, came to drop E and lose themselves in the sounds of techno, jungle, and hip-hop until the sun came up.

NASA had the same ravetastic spirit as Disco 2000, minus the sleazy, lurking weirdos. I rarely saw anyone old enough to vote, let alone buy a drink. If Disco 2000 was *The Lost Boys*, then NASA was *The Goonies* or *Lord of the Flies*—right before things went south and they started bashing each other with rocks. It wasn't entirely clear how one thousand underage kids were getting together weekly to roll and trip in the glorious confines of this massive compound, but who was I to question it? Mayor David Dinkins, who was busy tackling violent crime and a housing crisis, took a fairly laissez-faire approach to nightlife and underage clubbing. NASA didn't serve alcohol, so it was all ages—meaning no one checked ID at the door. But even at places that did sell drinks, like Limelight, bouncers didn't care much about how old we were. I had a terrible fake ID, a flimsy rectangle bought in a Times Square souvenir shop, where

I'd ducked into a back room and emerged seven years older, rechristened "Mark Jackson"—and I never had a problem. Even without an ID, a good story could get you past the door.

To outwit our parents and make our weekly pilgrimage to NASA, my friends Fred and Daniel and I would carefully coordinate sleepovers and rehearse meticulous backstories. This wasn't just another night out; this was Disneyland for serotonin-crazed youth. One February night, I left home in suede Puma sneaks and baggy X-Large jeans, looking innocent enough. My backpack held the real plan: ski goggles, Vicks VapoRub, and a handful of whistles—the rave tool kit.

Next, I met up with Alex Kane, my closest friend since moving from London. In fourth grade, his dad had died of a heart attack, leaving his mother—a loving Bronx Jew with fierce green eyes that could stare down a charging bull—to support their family alone. This also meant Alex's place became a hub for much unsupervised mischief. One time, Alex, Daniel, and I decided to mix an over-the-counter asthma medication with a two-dollar bottle of Boone's Farm white wine because some older kid swore it would get us drunk faster. Daniel ended up in the hospital, getting his stomach pumped.

We boarded the C train at Seventy-Second Street, a station whose wrought-iron railings spring from the Gothic Dakota like something out of a fairy tale, and emerged at Union Square, which looked more like the set of a zany public access TV show. We walked to Coffee Shop—the sceney Brazilian restaurant with a neon blue sign and tropical décor—and peeked inside, where beautiful people were being served by even more beautiful waiters. Rumor had it the hosts were told to seat the attractive customers up front.

Alex and I sat somewhere in the middle, sipping on our illegal screwdrivers.

After picking up Fred, we hopped a cab to the Shelter to join a few hundred teens in a line snaking around Hubert Street, almost to Greenwich. Everyone was bundled up in winter coats, blowing wisps of smoke into the cold air. The kid in front of us wore a Liquid Sky beanie pulled low, already pulling shapes to his own internal techno rhythm, his premature euphoria suggesting he took his drugs a little too early.

When we got past security and through the doors, the collective body heat of seven hundred sweaty adolescents transformed the Shelter's entrance into its own humid ecosystem. And once the E took hold, we all moved in slow motion through the thick atmosphere like mini astronauts shuffling along the surface of the moon.

Fred, in Bolle goggles with a yellow *Sesame Street* figure dangling from his neck, and Alex, in a low-cut white tank that flaunted his teenage man-fur, charged to the dance floor. Alex threw himself into the squelching synths, weaving his hands like an over-caffeinated shadow-puppeteer. I bobbed along but couldn't connect. The music was too fast and hard.

Groove lives in the space between a song's rhythmic elements, the way the horns and rhythm section of James Brown's "Cold Sweat" skip and stutter, causing that irresistible urge to move, like you literally have ants in your pants. But techno was relentlessly fast, with no room between accents. Just kick-kick-kick-kick. The unyielding, hypnotic pulse was perfect for getting lost on drugs, no distractions, just a trance-like state—as if staring into an abstract painting, you could make of it whatever you wanted. I looked around at hundreds of kids losing their minds, but I just couldn't fuck with it. I headed for the chill-out room for a techno-timeout.

I noticed a kid with a blue Afro and pretty, angular features that gave him an anime quality. His name came back to me—James—though everyone called him Blu Jemz because of the hair. He was the most interesting-looking person I'd ever seen.

"You're Blu Jemz, right?"

"Yeah," he replied, his smile lazy, his eyes fixed on some distant point. He was clearly somewhere else entirely. I flopped onto a circular sofa and a girl with pink hair sat on my lap and began to kiss me. Around us, a hundred other kids paired off in similar embraces, a PG-13 *Caligula* with glow sticks.

Super DJ Dmitry from Deee-Lite was in the back, spinning obscure disco I'd never heard. He threw on an up-tempo track with a filthy bass line. When the chorus hit, lush, jazzy piano chords poured in, and a female voice sweetly belted something about "Jamaica funk." I couldn't fathom being next door enduring an electronic anvil pounding into my brain while *this* was happening.

Suddenly, two kids pushed past, each carrying a milk crate filled with records. One of them, with shoulder-length blond hair, pulled out a pair of headphones and scanned the room like a cyborg. Dmitry stepped aside and the blond kid threw on his first record, Main Source's "Fakin' the Funk." As the intro gave way to the doo-wop fanfare of the sample, he pulled out a second copy, placed it on the other turntable, and scratched it in, thereby bringing the song back to the top, perfectly on beat. Dmitry's vibe had been open and inviting, like he was welcoming the room in for a hug; this blond kid, who couldn't have been much older than me, radiated a terrifying concentration, lording over the turntables like a sushi master at his cutting board.

As he tore through Black Moon, EPMD, and Double XX Posse, the room filled up quickly. A small circle gathered around the booth, with me front and center, watching his every move. He swapped records out in mere seconds, tossing them about with the perfect combination of grace and recklessness. Sometimes, he'd blend one track over another. Other times, he'd slam it in brutishly on beat. There was a dead seriousness in his eyes. As if losing a single dancing body from his grip was unacceptable.

He dropped "DWYCK," so perfectly the crowd let out a collective "Ohhhhh," like the sound that ripples through the West Fourth Street basketball courts after a killer crossover or a trick shot.

I pressed against the table that held his equipment, watching his hands, mouthing every word. When his last record finished, I asked his name.

"On-E," he replied. Me, too, I thought.

We got back to Fred's around 5:30 a.m., still flying. My mind kept replaying moments from On-E's performance.

Fred reached into one pocket of his Bear winter coat. As he checked the other pocket, his fumbling became more frantic.

"Oh, shit," he muttered. "My keys…"

Panic replaced all lingering euphoria. Our only option was to buzz up and wake his mom, who would certainly call my mother, which would mean an embargo on clubs and fun for the rest of the year. At least. Six months of successfully navigating curfews and fabricating alibis gone in an instant. Fred rang up. No answer. Shivering in his lobby, we knew we were screwed. To escape freezing to death, we trudged to McDonald's and slumped into the stiff plastic seats, passing a greasy hash brown back and forth, now painfully sober, while the workers behind the counter pointed and snickered at two strung-out teens wearing ski goggles and whistles. Fred's mom finally answered, reserved but furious, and promptly sent me home to trouble my own family.

My mother just glared at me. She had tolerated a lot of my teenage behavior. She understood the pull of night and my obsession with music. If she was worried, she rarely let on. The year before, I'd gotten a severe case of shingles that covered my torso when we had a gig at Wetlands. My guitar strap burned like fire against my skin. Midway through the set, I twisted too fast and winced in pain. When I caught my mother's eye in the crowd, she was fighting back tears. But she let me play. She knew stopping me would have hurt worse than the physical pain.

This time, though, I'd crossed the line. When I got home, she spared me the third degree, probably because I looked so wrecked. But when I woke up later, I got the full treatment—a master class in Jewish-mother guilting. I deserved it. For a week after, I stayed in my room as much as possible, ashamed to show my face.

Not long after, I was lying in bed trying to fall asleep when the heat pipes began clanging. It was the usual sound of a winter night in New York City. But this was different; sharper, almost deliberate. It only took a second clang, louder and more menacing, to know that I was hallucinating. This wasn't a natural sound—it had an anger to it. I shifted nervously under the covers, and the rustle of my sheets became an awful hiss.

The drip from the bathroom faucet thundered through my skull.

I turned on the radio, desperately hoping to break the spell. But the announcer's voice—usually a harmless, chipper drone—now seethed with spite as he read the weather. Every sound around me twisted into a horrific fun house mirror version of itself. And I was trapped inside.

Terrified, I got up and stumbled to my mother's door. "Mummy," I said, barely holding it together, "I think I'm having some sort of panic attack."

She appeared, half-asleep in her nightshirt. We weren't a family for hugs, but her voice came soft: "It's going to be okay." Those five words of mother's love made the terror start to drain. I stood for a moment in her gentle presence, and I headed back to bed.

I had a few more of those episodes that spring, always in the quiet dark. Since childhood, the night meant good times, so long as it was full of loud music and people. Emptied of that, it showed another side—paranoia, anxiety, and a darkness that could swallow you whole. Something I never wanted to face again. That's easy enough, I thought: Never be alone at night.

THREE

FROM THE OUTSIDE, Rock and Soul looked like any midtown electronics store—a jumble of shiny gadgets vying for attention amid the daily stampede of Seventh Avenue. But a second glance revealed this wasn't the usual lineup of Walkmans, cordless phones, and pagers.

Nope.

Gleaming in the window were names like Technics, Ortofon, UREI, Numark, and Odyssey, gear that purred, "Welcome, DJ. We've been expecting you." This was no place for tourists haggling over a camcorder. This was a temple, a sanctum for people with a calling. People like me—even if my "calling" was barely a year old. My mother, surrendering to my deepening obsession, had promised: Get into college, keep the raving under control, and she'd consider turntables for graduation. And now, here we were, in DJ nirvana.

Inside, only a bleary-eyed salesman occupied the store. *Right, real DJs don't do mornings!* The counters were crammed with every gadget a young selector could want: turntables, mixers, cartridges, amps, headphones, and soft carrying bags for transporting records to gigs. *Gigs!* I pictured myself marching into a house party with these bags in hand, ready to turn the place out.

I pointed out the Technics SL-1200s and Gemini Scratch Master mixer—the setup I'd been dreaming of for months. Before I could finish, she flipped into mom mode, grilling the salesman about the cheaper brands like she was moonlighting for *Consumer Reports*. A familiar heat washed over me, and suddenly I was back in fifth grade, standing in the schoolyard in Fayva discount high-tops while the kids circled me, pointing and laughing. My mom was married to a rock star, but growing up in a large family, she'd been impressed with the importance of buying for value. She believed American kids were too spoiled. Why spring for eighty-dollar Reeboks when Fayva's knockoffs cost half as much? Was she negotiating like a pro right now or trying to send me off to college with an ulcer? Who knew? I walked off to leave them be.

In the back, a carpeted stockroom turned record shop overflowed with bins labeled DISCO, HOUSE, R&B, REGGAE, and NEW RAP. After careful study, I chose "DWYCK," Redman's "Time 4 Sum Aksion," Digable Planets' "Rebirth of Slick (Cool Like Dat)," and Mary J. Blige's "Reminisce (Remix)." When I returned to the front, my mother had sealed the deal on the Technics. I hugged her with that teenage mix of pure gratitude and shameless groveling.

We hauled the mammoth boxes into the trunk of a cab and back to my room. Staples flew as I tore through the thick cardboard and protective sheets to reveal two gleaming, silver turntables nestled in Styrofoam thrones. Each was a plinth of steel and silver painted plastic, heavy as a small TV. The design was striking in its minimalism: die cast aluminum platter, 45 adapter, tonearm, and pitch-control slider. A series of clean, deliberate lines synonymous with DJing itself.

I took the second one out and set it on my desk. One turntable alone was a sight to behold. Two side by side constituted an art form. I screwed on the headshells with the Shure SC35 cartridges pre-mounted. A record is only a single spiraling groove, etched with microscopic wiggles that contain sound waves. The needle reads these vibrations like a decoder; its cartridge—with tiny magnets and coils—transforms mechanical movements into electrical signals. *That* then becomes music. Without the needle, a record is just a spiral spinning at 33⅓ revolutions per minute. Just as the inner ear transforms vibrations into music for the brain, a needle gives vinyl its voice.

Next, I got rid of the rubber mats that came with the turntables. Thick and weighty, like a drummer's practice pads, they were designed to stabilize the record and dampen low-end feedback. Perfect for audiophiles, useless for hip-hop DJing. I swapped them out for felt mats—thin, lightweight so I could have my way with a record.

I connected the red and white RCA cables to the Gemini Scratch Master, secured the grounding cables with their horseshoe clips, plugged in all three power cables, and flipped on my stereo. Finally, I placed Redman's "Time 4 Sum Aksion" on the right turntable, lifting the tonearm and carefully lowering the needle onto side A.

The speakers burst to life with one of the most glorious noises known to man, the sound of needle touching down to vinyl—like the moon landing for the ears, an electromagnetic connection followed by static, a low-end rumble, clicks, pops, then the orchestral burst of a sample from the Dramatics.

For three minutes, I watched the black and red label spin, mesmerized by its hypnotic rotation, and then the stark reality hit me: I had zero idea what to do next. Beyond listening to Stretch Armstrong and Funkmaster Flex on the radio, and observing DJs at raves while off my face, I had no knowledge of how any of this actually worked. Not a clue.

Fuck it, everyone has to start somewhere.

I pulled the Mary J. Blige record from its plastic sleeve, placed it on the other turntable, and slipped on my headphones for my inaugural attempt at beat-matching—the fundamental technique of aligning the tempo of two songs so they can play together at the same time. But I dropped the needle and it skidded off like a car careening over a cliff, producing a horrifying sound as it scraped against the metal platter. I inspected the needle, praying it wasn't ruined. On my second attempt, I dropped the tonearm too quickly, and the needle bounced wildly, up and down, like a chopper trying to land in a monsoon.

I understood rhythm enough to know I'd have to locate the downbeat—or "beat one"—of Mary's song in the headphones. But I could never stop it in exactly the right place with my hand. When I tried rewinding the record with the needle down—the DJ technique called backcueing—I knocked the tonearm with the edge of my palm, sending it flying off the platter. Other times, the heavy torque of the Technics' direct-drive motor fought against my every move. And then came the challenge of listening to two records at once—one in my headphones and one from the speakers. Did DJs grow second brains for this? Hours of trying to cue Mary in the phones and release at the perfect moment got me maybe two seconds of sync before Mary and Redman veered horribly off course. The misaligned beats found endless ways to career into one another, like two drunk runners tripping over each other on a track.

But each mistake was a reason to try again.

After days of repeating the same blends—easy enough with only four records—that second brain started growing. My hands steadied. I learned to rewind the record without knocking shit every which way. And I started to get the hang of the pitch control—a slider that moves like a dimmer switch, nudging the record from slow to fast and vice versa—the most important tool for keeping two records aligned.

Daniel dropped by after school. While button-mashing the shit out of *Street Fighter II*, he turned and asked, "So can you, like, scratch or anything yet?"

"Kind of," I mumbled, moving my hand back and forth on the record, producing a sound that impressed neither of us. He bailed to pummel Chun-Li in the quiet comfort of his own apartment.

My basic eight-bar blends weren't going to wow anyone. To pull off the tricks I heard Stretch Armstrong nail, I needed help.

* * *

"Hi, is Manny there?"

"Yeah, this is Manny…"

"I don't know if you remember me, but my name's Mark Ronson, I go to Collegiate…"

Manny Ames had radiated a B-boy swagger unlike anyone

34

who'd attended our buttoned-up school. Three years older, the Peruvian-Italian teen once posted up in the playground in his Adidas Top Tens, sporting stubble and an oversized bomber jacket, while we pipsqueaks scurried past in peach fuzz and blazers with elbow patches. And he DJed.

"You had that weird blond streak?" he asked, referencing the peroxide stripe my mother made me dye into my hair for my Bar Mitzvah so I wouldn't look "boring." Most kids stopped me in the hallway to ask if pigeons had crapped on my head.

"That's me…" I said, deciding to take it as an identifier, not an insult. "Anyway, I just got turntables and want to DJ, I remembered you did, and I was hoping to get some lessons?"

"Hmmmm, I'm pretty busy," he said in a way that implied he wasn't. "How'd you get my number again?"

"I stole it from the alumni office."

"Okay," he said, a new hint of respect in his voice. "Tell me what you know about DJing."

"Well, I listen to Stretch Armstrong every week."

"You know Stretch went to Collegiate, right?"

What?! Stretch Armstrong, rap radio legend, had gone to *our* school?!

"No way."

"Yeah, Stretch Armstrong is Adrian Bartos, class of '87."

I remembered Adrian Bartos—tall, lanky, with glasses. But Adrian Bartos was *white*. I'd only heard Stretch on radio, that cool deep baritone—he couldn't be white.

"I remember Adrian Bartos, but he was, is…um…white," I said.

"Yeah, B, Adrian Bartos is white. So is Stretch Armstrong. Same guy."

"Oh…" I said. *What an idiot.*

"All right, I'll show you some stuff," he said. "Make sure you have two copies of the same record."

I went back to Rock and Soul and bought a second copy of Redman, and two days later, Manny showed up, ready to teach.

I led him through our apartment, now a maze of moving boxes. We'd been forced to sell the place—furniture, belongings, everything—after a trusted advisor embezzled tens of millions of dollars from Mick. In the aftermath, Mick sank deep into depression, barely leaving the apartment for six months.

Before his success, Mick spent decades bouncing between cult bands such as Nero and the Gladiators and Spooky Tooth—a hired gun, scraping by. In 1977, he formed Foreigner, self-financed some demos, and was rejected by every A&R guy in the business except one, John Kalodner at Atlantic Records. Then Foreigner hit it bigger than he ever could have imagined, and for fifteen years, remained a huge success. Now, he'd just lost everything. My mother had some money saved from the divorce from my father—enough to get us into a rental uptown while Mick figured out how to start over. She kept a brave face, but some nights, I heard the same fierce arguments through her door that had marked my parents' marriage. In the safety of my room, Manny dropped his bag and got to work.

"All right. To rock doubles, you need to mark up your records," he said, suddenly adopting the gravitas of a Technics general. He slapped a copy of Redman on each turntable and without looking pulled one back and forth, creating a tough *jhugga jhugga* sound.

"You got any stickers?"

I scrambled for some Maxell cassette labels. He peeled them off casually and showed me how to mark up two copies of the same record by attaching the sticker from the center hole outward, like the needle on a compass.

"This way you'll always know where you are visually while you're running two records back and forth," he said, sharing something both straightforward and mind-blowing.

The stickers allowed him to spin the record back to precise spots—2 o'clock, 7 o'clock, etc.—by tracking each revolution of the disc. Each position on the clock face corresponded to a specific sound: the kick drum might be at 3 o'clock, the snare hit at 9 o'clock, making it possible to consistently find and repeat any part of the beat.

In doing so, Manny was channeling techniques Grandmaster Flash had invented fifteen years earlier. Before Flash, DJ Kool Herc's "Merry-Go-Round" method pioneered extending the break—the section of a song that electrified dancers—by using two copies of the same record. Herc would keep the energy flowing, switching between identical records to prolong the most dynamic moment of the track. Flash then perfected it, using headphones to precisely cue the identical section of the record on the second turntable while the first break played through the speakers. When the break ended, he'd switch seamlessly to the cued section, locking it perfectly on beat and repeating the loop to create two-, four-, or eight-bar cycles for as long as he wanted.

For the next two weeks, I practiced relentlessly, only emerging for school and dinner. My bedroom, situated at the end of a long hallway, far from the others, provided welcome isolation, allowing me to escape the emotional turbulence elsewhere in the house.

One evening, I stepped out to find Mike Heller—an irrepressibly jovial friend of my sisters who spent so much time at our house that the doorman assumed he was another sibling—camped out in the kitchen.

"My cousin Phil does parties," Mike said. "He needs a DJ and he's into rap and stuff, so I told him about you."

"Did you tell him I've only been DJing for, like, five weeks?"

"Five, six, whatever!" he said, with a concerning amount of confidence. "You're gonna kill it!"

I called cousin Phil, who was, in fact, uneasy with my limited credentials. Fortunately for me, he had no backup plan. So, on a snowy Wednesday night in March, I piled my turntables, mixer, half a crate of records, and a backpack full of cables into a yellow Crown Vic cab that sloshed through icy gray puddles en route to a dive on the Upper East Side called Jungle Jim's. I lugged each piece through to a back room, where a small, elevated platform draped in white fringe stood—atop it was a rickety table with skinny metal legs, the first of many that would mark my life. Once I set up my turntables and mixer and plugged up all my RCA cables, the soundman patched me into the PA.

The O'Jays' "For the Love of Money" broke the silence. I remember learning from Mick in his studio that the song's huge, spacious sound stemmed from recording engineer Joe Tarsia's innovative use of reverb. What made the track distinctive was how Tarsia dynamically controlled this effect, abruptly switching the reverb from full to none, creating the sensation of being transported from a giant cathedral into an intimate, close-walled room.

After recording the "Money money money" vocal hook, he flipped the reel-to-reel tape so that it played backwards—a technique from the sixties—creating a surreal sucking effect. These ground-breaking manipulations of space and sound had always impressed me, but hearing them blasting through Jungle Jim's PA system was an entirely different experience: magnificent and funky as hell.

My favorite records, filling the entire space. I liked this feeling.

I glanced at the bartender wiping down the counter. His movements seemed energized. Was it from me?

Thirty high school hip-hoppers with nothing better to do trickled in that night, wrapped in oversized Avirex jackets and teen swagger. Nothing I'd practiced at home prepared me for the nerves of playing live, though. When a blend went off beat in my bedroom, I'd calmly course-correct. But here, in front of these kids, panic took over. I couldn't discern which track was ahead, which was behind, mistakenly giving the record a gentle push to speed it up, when it was already ahead.

It was incredible to be playing music at this volume, but it also made the headphones harder to hear. I got thrown off easily and had to crash-land a few mixes.

There were a couple of bright spots, and when I dropped Wu-Tang's "Protect Ya Neck"—the biggest underground record of the moment—the room came together for three minutes like a pulsing swarm. But the night was, for the most part, a flop.

Phil wasn't discouraged. He had his next one lined up: Friday nights at the Surf Club, a two-story relic on East Ninety-First all the way over by the river. Back in the eighties, after Studio 54 shut down, the Surf Club had a brush with hipness—Rick James had gotten super-freaky there, probably doing bumps with debutantes. Now it was hanging by a thread and happy to turn a blind eye to underage kids throwing parties.

The regular DJs played whatever was on MTV, basically George Michael's "Faith" on repeat. Phil, though, had hung out at real hip-hop spots like Mars and Tunnel, and was set on bringing that vibe to the prep schoolers. He called to say I had the gig; he just needed my DJ name for the flyer.

A name? I had no good nicknames to draw from. Only "Commie" and "Wrong Way Ronson," thanks to a humiliating mishap in the four-hundred-meter relay at Field Day that still haunted me. Neither screamed legend—more like "Please stuff me in a locker." On the spot, I blurted out "DJ Olde English," a nod to my UK roots and the malt liquor that you'd buy at bodegas in bottles big enough to use as free weights. Armed with three hundred cardboard flyers announcing my dumb name, Phil and I hit the Meadow, passing them out to crusties, hip-hop heads, and a couple of confused hot-dog vendors.

Back home, I holed up in my room, hunched over my Technics, preparing. By now, I had about fifty records, including a dozen old soul and funk LPs I'd grabbed from Mick's music room. I practiced every combination to find blends that worked. Every record got tapped out on a Boss Dr. Beat metronome, its BPM carefully written on a stickie label and pasted on the record cover.

While fucking around with Cypress Hill's "How I Could Just Kill a Man," I had an idea.

Hummin', comin' atcha / And you know I had to gat'cha! / Time for some action...

Redman had sampled that line on "Time 4 Sum Aksion," adding a digital stutter: *time-time-for some / time for some action.* The thread was there across both tracks. I just had to sew them together.

So, I practiced a blend to stitch the Cypress Hill record into Redman's stuttered hook, adjusting tempos and tweaking transitions to make it sound as if Redman was finishing Cypress Hill's thought.

That Friday, I rolled up to the Surf Club half an hour before opening, surprised to see a few dozen people already lined up outside. Phil had bombed every school in the city with flyers, and miraculously the weather gods hadn't dumped another snowstorm on us. Maybe this was going to pop off?

I carried my crates up the stairs to the booth. A real booth, with a door and everything. The architect must have been channeling cubist Picasso—the window was positioned at such an angle that it offered no view of the dance floor. All night, I had to keep opening the door and sticking my head out like a teenage cuckoo clock to check the floor. But it was a legit booth, with compressors, crossovers, and bins to place records—a step up from Jungle Jim's shaky plastic table.

By 10:00 p.m., it was packed—prep, public, and Catholic school kids, a hurricane of hormones and CK One, out on the floor. White girls in tight jeans and ribbed tank tops shouted the words to A Tribe Called Quest's "Scenario," featuring Busta Rhymes, like they'd been possessed by the spirit of Busta himself. My Cypress Hill/Redman mix drew a collective "Ohhhhh!"—the same reaction I'd given On-E that night at NASA. Inside my little closet sanctuary, with its tattered polyester carpet underfoot and a monitor wedge blasting up like a hundred tinny clock radios, the feeling of validation beat anything I'd ever felt onstage with my band.

Five hours passed in a flash. At closing time, they flicked on the house lights. I was coated in sweat, and my record covers were sticking out at every angle. The place was deserted like I'd been at a party with three hundred friends, turned around for a second, and everyone had vanished without saying goodbye. A mix of triumph and loneliness hit at the same time. I needed it to be next Friday already, so I could do it all over again.

Not long after I started booking gigs, I met Amanda, who lived with her family in our new building. Her father was Peter Gatien—the "Club King"—who owned Limelight, Palladium, and Tunnel. He was the most important figure in New York nightlife and famously wore a patch over one eye, which only added to his mystique. Amanda had convinced him to let her throw a weekly Thursday party at Club USA in Times Square. She asked me to DJ and hired two savvy high school promoters, Jason Strauss and Noah Tepperberg.

For most DJs, getting into Gatien's clubs meant years of playing tiny bars and dimly lit backrooms before earning a spot at Club USA. I should have needed that long—building connections, making my way up gradually. Instead, I stumbled right into it. I already had advantages that most others didn't. My mother bought me the gear. I was raised by a musician with a home studio. But this was an absurdly lucky break, even for me. The thought of playing Club USA was surreal. I felt way too green for such a big stage. But no way was I turning it down.

Gatien's clubs each had their own personality. Limelight had Gothic drama; Palladium brought futuristic interiors to an erstwhile movie palace; Tunnel was a cavernous industrial playground. But Club USA, in the theater district, was the ultimate spectacle—the unholy love child of Broadway camp and Times Square sleaze.

The four-story building, a converted theater on West Forty-Seventh Street, occupied a block otherwise dominated by parking garages, Broadway theaters, and pizza joints only a tourist or starving stagehand could love. Upon entering, a deep, S&M-tinged voice declared, "Welcome to Club USA," an admonition to check all moral judgment at the door. The club's centerpiece was a three-story indoor slide that snaked through the main room and deposited patrons onto the dance floor—often with fewer articles of clothing than they had begun with.

Then there were the money drops—ten thousand dollars in cash. People clawed the sky as Benjamins fluttered down in a drug-fueled parody of the American dream. Go-go dancers perched on massive podiums; one girl famously shot milk from her breast into the crowd. The bathrooms were their own party. The photo booths doubled as blow job havens.

At the top of it all was the Mugler Room, a tall annex that served as a chic, industrial hang zone with a steady stream of people flowing in and out. I climbed a thirty-foot steel staircase to the DJ booth. Looking down, my stomach dropped and I gripped the railing. I hated heights, and this was like DJing from an overpass above the Long Island Expressway.

Everything was shaking up here on this precarious structure, including the turntables, which were suspended by rubber bands to isolate them from floor-shaking bass vibrations, which would otherwise cause terrible feedback. The rubber band suspension worked for house-music DJs, who created long, gradual transitions between tracks, and required minimal touching of the turntables once the beats were synchronized. But for hip-hop, it was a nightmare. Hip-hop technique demands quick transitions, scratching, and frequently backcueing. Any of these actions sent the decks wobbling unpredictably, like pressing down on a motel waterbed. I improvised a solution by cramming cocktail napkins into the gaps between the turntable platters and their bases to lessen the movement. It wasn't pretty, but it worked.

I dropped Mary J. Blige and surveyed the room from my perch. The Mugler had no dance floor, which made it hard to get anything going. I got two people dancing, then focused on them. Soon, two more joined—then four, then a dozen. But at some point, I played the wrong tune, and everyone scattered.

Watching the high school kids mingle with the Club Kids was like a National Geographic special: *Observe the courtship dance of the female clubber, heavily pierced and adorned with a sheer green bodysuit, as she tugs playfully on the bowling shirt of an adolescent male who was previously observed being instructed to stay home and pack for college.*

For the whole night, the crowd was in transit, passing from the main room to the VIP room to the side and back to the Mugler. Holding their attention was nearly impossible. I'd get them for a few songs, then lose them again. My usual set struggled to land—hip-hop and funk grooves were getting swallowed by the towering sixty-foot ceilings. This—music fighting architecture—was an age-old problem. The reverberant acoustics of churches, which, in the Middle Ages, were getting taller and taller, had long dictated what could be performed there. These enormous spaces, with their pro-longed reverberation times, caused sounds to linger and blend, forcing composers to avoid complex modulations that would have turned into a chaotic mess played live. Eight hundred years later, I was fighting the same acoustic battle. On top of that, the hedonist energy of the Mugler craved lobotomizing beats, not the soulful pleas of the Jackson 5.

By 2:00 a.m., the floor vanished entirely. Nothing I could do would hold them. I was despondent. Amanda had given me a huge chance and I was blowing it. But there was still time to adjust and save face as I was already booked to play for the next few weeks. So, the next day, I went to Rock and Soul to fix my rookie fuck-up.

I asked the house music specialist for the five biggest club records. He handed me Jaydee's "Plastic Dreams," the Good Men's "Give It Up," Robin S.'s "Show Me Love," Crystal Waters's "Gypsy Woman," and Masters at Work featuring India's "I Can't Get No Sleep."

The following week, when the energy started to dip around 1:00 a.m., I dropped my new selections and witnessed the magic that these records worked in a room like this, appreciating up-tempo electronic music in a way I never had back at NASA. Maybe I'd been listening wrong. Maybe I hadn't been listening at all. India's soaring vocal on "I Can't Get No Sleep" was as soulful and gripping as any disco classic. The drums on the Good Men's "Give It Up" thundered like a Brazilian Carnival. The hypnotic power of these songs—locked in one key, powered by metallic drums—was made for spaces like this. Watching what it did to two hundred bodies, feeling their communal lift, made me love them even more. I watched the room. No exodus this time.

At 3:00 a.m., I handed off to the next DJ. Unlike Surf Club, which would've been closed by then, the Mugler was still buzzing. I'd been up in my tower since midnight, totally sober, and needed to catch up quick. I found a friend with coke, and we headed straight to a bathroom stall, the phantom taste of the drip in my throat before he could even cut a line.

I played Club USA every Thursday that summer. At the end of August, Amanda and I had our last hurrah and stayed out all night. As the sun came up, I loaded her into a car headed to the airport, bound for USC. I was headed to Vassar College in a week. But in that moment, I had no real idea why. New York had just given me a glimpse of who I could be.

FOUR

"DO WE TAKE the Taconic or Route 9?" I asked, wrestling with a mangled map of New York State.

"Lena said to take the Taconic," my mother replied, referring to her psychic healer.

"Lena lives in Poughkeepsie?"

"No, but she *is* a psychic, so I asked her where there'd be less traffic," she said brightly.

"Isn't that a violation of her spiritual powers?"

She ignored the question and turned on her favorite station, WNEW classic rock. "Paint It Black" was on.

"You know, I always liked the Rolling Stones more than the Beatles," she said, as if confessing a dirty secret.

"How is that even possible?! The Beatles have such better songs. Plus, you're from *Liverpool*!"

"I don't know, they were always a bit more naughty," she said, raising an eyebrow.

I groaned. Naughty?! My mother loved to stay up late, but she wasn't naughty. Or, if she was, I wanted to know nothing more about it. As a kid, whenever I wandered out into the party, there she was—champagne glass in hand, tuned in completely to whoever she was talking to. She hung on their every word, displaying a preternatural empathy. People loved confiding in her. She listened in a way that made them feel seen. Her friends would show up to our apartment frazzled, shaking, and tearful, only to leave in the wee hours of the morning, a little buzzed but utterly restored.

I stared out at the Taconic—clear as the cloudless sky.

Lena was the highway whisperer after all.

We were on our way up to Vassar College for freshman orientation. Truth be told, I didn't mind leaving the city for a bit. I'd return—I already felt I was a Manhattan lifer destined to be buried in one of those giant Jewish cemeteries out by JFK. What were four years away in the grand scheme of things?

We pulled onto campus. It was gorgeous: ancient elms, pristine lawns, and red-brick buildings with pointed arches and rows and rows of windows.

My mother had taken me to some breathtaking places in my life—Ibiza, Saint Martin, the South of France—and yet here we were, peering out like Columbus approaching the Americas. It wasn't the place itself, but what it represented. There was a sense of discovery, of independence and adventure—and the promise of a train that could get me to Grand Central in two hours flat.

I lugged the records and she schlepped a cardboard box of clothes up the stairs into a musty, sunlit dorm room still smelling like fresh paint. She stood in the middle of the room, proud of me and maybe a little proud of herself, too. She'd had no role model for raising a family. Yet here she was, managing to get one full-grown teenager out the door and off to college in decent working condition.

Alex and his mom arrived moments later. They were closer than any other mother-son I knew. We'd been best friends for a decade, and now college roommates. Our mothers helped us make our beds one last time, hugged us goodbye, and then set out back to the city. Before either car hit the Taconic, Alex was unpacking his three-foot bong. A sophomore named Tony, who lived down the hall, popped his head in and handed us two tabs of acid, which we dropped without hesitation. Twenty-four hours later, I woke up, worse for wear, staring at walls covered in my own Sharpie scrawl: all four verses of Eric B. & Rakim's "I Know You Got Soul."

I quickly learned that Vassar was crawling with so many DJs I could toss a slip mat out my window and hit one. There were Chicago house heads, Detroit techno fiends, snooty experts on New York dance classics. And reigning supreme was Ben Velez, the undisputed authority on rare groove, jazz, funk, and soul.

Ben was an enigma. He perched in trees reading the *Tao Te Ching*, his blond dreads tied in a Rasta crown, sandalwood burning beside him. Wave to him, and he'd wave back without breaking his balance. There were rumors that he studied teleportation, though no one could confirm. A militant socialist on full scholarship, he stayed clear of the pampered parade of Vassar students and kept to a small circle of friends.

It took a month of trailing Ben around campus to earn his trust. But before long, I sat cross-legged on the tatty carpet of his dorm room, the sunlight streaming through the windows backlighting him like some dreadlocked vinyl Jesus.

I was spellbound by Ben's collection of rare records. Hip-hop not only brought me to DJing, it also put me on to the sixties and seventies records that provided "the breaks"—or samples—that formed its foundation.

Hip-hop in the eighties drew on familiar source material: James Brown, Chic, Aerosmith, Otis Redding. But as it evolved, producers like Q-Tip and Large Professor began digging for more obscure records—not only jazz and soul but psychedelia and prog rock—with richer textures and a wider sonic palette. Plus, the rarer the record, the less chance someone else would sample it first.

My love for A Tribe Called Quest and Gang Starr led me down a rabbit hole of artists like Ronnie Laws, Brian Auger's Oblivion Express, Young-Holt Unlimited, and Grant Green. I didn't have the money for those records or the know-how to track them down, so, back in New York, I sought out the DJs who played them.

I found Soul Kitchen, a Monday night party with DJ Frankie Inglese—a Jersey-bred New Yorker who'd started sneaking into Xenon, the legendary Manhattan disco, at fifteen. There, the resident DJ spotted transfixed Frankie and invited him into the booth, sparking his lifelong obsession with vinyl and moving crowds. Ten years later, he and Jack Luber, his partner in crime, had the biggest soul party downtown. Pete Rock rapped about it; Naomi Campbell and a thousand others hung out there.

At some point, Anthony Bourdain, a Soul Kitchen regular, connected with Jack and Frankie while working as head chef at the Supper Club in midtown—a deco ballroom next to the old Edison Hotel, with engraved carpets, towering ceilings, and huge chandeliers. This was several years before Bourdain's brilliant memoir, *Kitchen Confidential*, turned him into a cultural phenomenon. In the evenings, the place served upscale martini-guzzling diners, but Bourdain convinced the owner to give Jack and Frankie the space after hours. At these parties, I'd stand alone all night, listening to Frankie spin RAMP, Rasputin's Stash, and Kool & the Gang. Outside of Soul Kitchen, I had no other way of hearing these tunes—until I met Ben.

Back in his dorm room, Ben pulled a record from the stash: a man in John Lennon glasses lying in a field, blowing into a tenor sax. The title, in swirling sixties bubble letters, read *The Honeysuckle Breeze*, by Tom Scott. He set it on his Technics and adjusted the volume on his GLI mixer—a jet-black cinder block, revered by old-school purists for being the first with a crossfader. And because nostalgia favors the most unwieldy.

The needle touched down and a twelve-string guitar emerged, playing a wistful descending line reminiscent of the Beatles' "Dear Prudence." For ninety seconds, it was just a lovely piece of melancholy folk music. Then Tom Scott's saxophone burst in with its sputtering phrasing, and my world cracked open. Between the sax, the descending bass line, and the ethereal oohs and aahs, I felt the floor disappear beneath me. This was it: the original sample for Pete Rock & C.L. Smooth's "They Reminisce over You (T.R.O.Y.)"—even more haunting and beautiful in its virgin form.

I became a fixture in Ben's room, peeking through his window to see if he was in, then taking a seat on the floor and soaking up his gospel of Bobbi Humphrey, Patrice Rushen, and Ronnie Foster. His records were the Rosetta stone of hip-hop, the key to deciphering the original language. He spoke of Japanese dealers and record fairs teeming with diggers and collectors while I sat absorbing every word he spoke.

You could say it was my first seminal class at school.

THE SACRED ART OF VINYL

INSTRUCTOR: Professor Ben Velez, Senior (Class of '95), Vinyl Jesus in Perpetuum

COURSE LOCATION: Ben's room in Main Building

COURSE DESCRIPTION: Over the course of two semesters, students will learn about the ancient language of hip-hop samples—the bass and horn lines that birthed some of the most revolutionary music being crafted in America today. All are welcome to apply, but only the highest-ranking beat junkies who exhibit an exceptional degree of trustworthiness and pure intentions will be selected. As part of the course, Professor Velez, a record archaeologist and esteemed authority on rare breaks, will provide access to what has been determined to be one of the illest record collections in the region.

In the ear-sharpening unit, students will learn to identify samples after a single vibraphone note, avoiding novice mistakes like blurting out, "Oh, I know this from Biggie." Lectures on the origins of the GLI crossfader will be accompanied by supervised practice sessions, with bonus points awarded for carrying the equipment, which is roughly the weight of a cinder block, across the quad. Finally, students will be instructed on how to navigate the shadowy underworld of record fairs and mysterious Japanese vinyl dealers, cultivating a monk-like patience to unearth hidden gems.

In sum, motivated students will learn the delicate balance of the vinyl cosmos, building a capacity to not only listen to records, but experience them as revelations. This is a graduate-level seminar.

I scored well in Ben's class. And while he rarely DJed outside of his room, deeming most Vassar students unworthy of his hard-won selections, I was the opposite—imposing my tastes on anyone with ears. Dorm rooms; house parties; the school radio station, WVKR—I was there, turntables in tow. But the holy grail was the Mug, a student-run basement club hidden below Main Building. On a campus swarming with DJs, a slot at the Mug only opened when someone graduated, got kicked out, or keeled over. My reputation was growing, though, and when the Wednesday night resident DJ was laid low by either *E. coli* or a weed cookie (I didn't ask), Tamar Tate, the junior who ran the night, called me in.

The Mug was a plain black box with a wooden bar, a dance floor in the middle, and a DJ setup so in the middle of it all, you could high-five half the dancers. Basement parties always go off. Everything feels hotter down below. There's something primal about descending underground, as if everyone's been summoned for a Dionysian rite.

This, combined with all the daylight pressures—exams, student loans, the existential dread about what you're even going to *do* with that English degree, anyway—it was a foolproof recipe for unhinged catharsis.

The Mug was my second class.

BASEMENT PARTY 101

INSTRUCTORS:

- Professor Tamar Tate, Junior (Class of '95)
- DJ Ease & DJ Paul Nice (off-campus legends)
- Pretty much everyone who walks through the door

COURSE LOCATION: The Mug, Main Building

COURSE DESCRIPTION: The classroom for this course— a black-box performance space in Main Building, ten feet below where Edna St. Vincent Millay once redefined the feminist voice—is itself part of the curriculum. This is the Mug: the underground heartbeat of Vassar's nightlife, its wooden bar teeming with students shaking off anxiety to the neck-snapping G-funk of tracks such as "Afro Puffs," by the Lady of Rage.

Professor Tate is a veteran of New York City venues such as Tunnel, Sheets and Pillows, and wherever else her fake ID could take her. In lectures, she will dive deep into the roots of funk, soul, and R&B. In follow-up seminars, students will learn how to weave seventies and eighties classics such as "Outstanding," by the Gap Band; "All Night Long," by the Mary Jane Girls; "Best of My Love," by the Emotions; and "Got to Be Real," by Cheryl Lynn, into era-spanning sets.

NIGHT PEOPLE

Poughkeepsie's own local legends DJ Ease and Paul Nice will lead the party-science unit, walking students through the New York style of crafting a night:

- Starting with funk and R&B classics.
- Easing into old-school hip-hop by Big Daddy Kane, Biz Markie, and Slick Rick.
- Setting the room alight with Method Man and new school heat.
- Taking it to dancehall with Buju Banton.
- Bringing it back to classics.
- Capping the night with slow jams, giving even the shyest wallflowers their last chance to hook up.

This course will teach students how to harness the raw, unhinged energy of an underground college rager. From coaxing that first brave soul to set down their Dixie cup and hit the dance floor, to dodging falling asbestos when Kingsley, the Jamaican manager, pounds the wall in approval for Sister Nancy's "Bam Bam," the class will learn how to transform any chaotic, sweaty party into an unforgettable night.

Performance reviews will be graded with high expectations. Students expecting to play sets that impressed the scrunchy-wearing, L.L. Bean–adorned kids from their hometown will be disappointed. Passing the exam requires more than coasting by on "O.P.P." or "Insane in the Brain." The Mug is a crucible of taste.

I did well in this class, too. If I played it right, no one left the Mug until Tamar rang the closing bell. One night, we were climbing the stairs, exhilarated and sweaty, and she asked, "How do you *do that* to everybody?" I shrugged. I didn't feel like saying, "Because I have this weird knack for reading people, I need to be in control, and I kind of love the attention that comes with it."

The Mug made me an immeasurably better DJ. Those thousand hours playing old disco records and learning their fluctuating tempos were essential. The drummers in the sixties and seventies were tight, but they weren't computer precise—they naturally drifted. Records like "Got to Be Real" or War's "Galaxy" might speed up in places, and when you're blending them with another track, you need to know exactly where those spots are so you can anticipate and adjust—with either the pitch control or your hands. This knowledge only came from playing these records night after night.

Back home, I'd been playing music to kids my age or younger. Now, I was playing for a mixed crowd, older and more in the know than me, who weren't shy to point out the gaps in my knowledge. So I made pilgrimages to the city, hunting down old school—Special Ed, Dana Dane, and Boogie Down Productions.

One afternoon, I was headed to Rock and Soul when a woman stopped me on the street and sent me to an open casting for a Calvin Klein ad. When I got there, I made friends with two male models in baggy jeans named Ethan Browne and Simon Rex. Ethan had the sharp cheekbones of his mother, a model named Phyllis Major, and the soulful eyes of his father, Jackson Browne—the singer-songwriter and Laurel Canyon heartthrob. (They met soon after Browne broke up with Joni Mitchell.) Simon grew up in the Bay Area, where he had dabbled in modeling after graduating high school. At twenty-one, with not much else going on, he scraped together enough for a one-way ticket to Milan, where he landed a few fashion shows. That was where he met Ethan, who took him under his wing, got him signed to Boss Models, and landed him a spot in a Tommy Hilfiger campaign.

Ethan said that he DJed, and after the casting we all went back to the apartment they shared, east of Union Square. The place was barren except for a black leather couch, a few crates of records, and a plastic table precariously holding turntables. The décor screamed "soulless bachelor pad," but also "independence." I could hardly believe two kids near my age had their own digs. Ethan rolled a massive blunt and motioned for me to jump on the decks.

Getting on someone else's turntables for the first time is like cooking in a stranger's kitchen. You have no idea where anything is, you're scared to touch the good knives, and you're certain that you'll accidentally set the place on fire. Yet you're expected to serve up something impressive enough to delight everyone—I threw on Jeru the Damaja and left it at that.

"I'm DJing this model party at Flowers tonight," Ethan said, as I subtly dodged an atomic plume of smoke coming from his mouth. I liked drugs, but mostly uppers. Weed made me dopey and paranoid; a cloud of this size would send me to St. Vincent's.

"You want to roll with us?"

"Model party" was one of the most vapid nightlife terms I'd ever heard. Of course, I immediately said yes.

Flowers turned out to be a dimly lit, moody lounge with leather love seats adorned by a bunch of pretty twenty-somethings. Like a DKNY campaign shot in Wayne Manor. Ethan was set up on a plastic table in the back, playing Kool & the Gang's "Hollywood Swinging."

"Yo, take over for a sec. I have to piss."

With those words, a DJ duo was born.

When Ethan came back, we traded off all night and planned our own party. He knew Roy Liebenthal, the owner of Café Tabac, which, back then, felt like the trendiest restaurant on earth. I'd never been but had heard plenty of stories: Kate Moss met Johnny Depp there, and Bono hung out and poured his own Guinness behind the bar.

I called Ethan from the dorm pay phone a few days later.

"I got Tabac," he said.

"Amazing! When do we start? This Friday?!"

"Nah, Roy would only give us a Monday."

Eesh. I had sociology on Tuesdays. I didn't drive, and the last train to Poughkeepsie would be leaving before I'd even arrived at the bar. Getting back for class would be impossible. And it was the one academic class that I liked. Ms. Harriford, my professor, was sharp and inspiring, the kind of person who'd make you want to graduate and open a sociology store, or whatever it was that sociologists did.

Still, Ethan and Tabac had their own allure, and Café Tabac beckoned.

"See you Monday, bro," I said.

* * *

Café Tabac so resembled a 1930s Belgian bistro, you half expected someone to burst in shouting, "*Listen up, everyone! They've invaded Poland!*" Every detail was spot on, from the vintage lighting to the herringbone-tiled floors. Upstairs, there was a private lounge with a handsome bar, banquettes upholstered in seafoam leather, and a blood-red velvet pool table.

It also taught me an invaluable New York lesson: the chicer the spot, the more bullshit the DJ setup. And Café Tabac was the chicest of all.

We were instructed to set up our equipment at the end of the wooden bar upstairs. The steel turntables atop the old-world, weathered surface would have made for a vibey aesthetic, if we weren't stationed directly in front of the espresso machine. Every ten minutes, an overworked busboy would barrel through, face locked in a grimace, arms loaded with coffee beans and cups. To make way, Ethan and I had to contort ourselves to take up the least amount of space possible, our hands clutching the edge of the bar.

Lounge gigs are fun. With no pressure to make people dance, you're just playing records to show the world how cool you are. We'd spin Gang Starr's "Mass Appeal," album cuts from the Pharcyde, and Black Moon's "I Got Cha Opin (Remix)" into Barry White's "Playing Your Game, Baby," the song it sampled. Supermodels like Bridget Hall and Milla Jovovich shot pool while chic fashionistas—twice my age—lounged around, sipping cocktails and looking glamorous.

And, inevitably, mid-set, I'd spot my mother gliding through the room—because in this downtown fashion world that I was just starting to discover, she'd been partying with half the room since I was in middle school.

One Monday, she walked up as Ethan was bent over, taking a hit between tunes. He stood up, exhaling gray smoke, and offered her the bong. "Thank you, darling, but I prefer uppers," she said. Apple, meet tree.

City gigs started trickling in—another lounge, high school reunion parties on holiday weekends, and a hip-hop open mic night at AKA on East Houston that came to a dramatic end when one rapper pulled a gun onstage after a punch line hit too close to home. I was right behind them, and dove behind the turntables as the sparse crowd bolted for the door. After a while, the Metro-North commute began to wear on me. Especially in the winter, catching the last train from Poughkeepsie, when I was often the only passenger in the car. Burnt out, I'd sit with my head bouncing against the cold glass, trying to snatch a disco nap. When we got to Grand Central Station, I hauled two crates of records through the cavernous halls like Paddington Bear en route to a rave. The morning return wasn't much better. I'd wrestle my crates on board a packed train, stack them in the aisle, and perch on them like a bleary-eyed gargoyle.

One ride, I felt a stabbing pain in my stomach—so intense I doubled over. Drenched in sweat, certain that something inside me had ruptured, I was freaked out. It lasted half an hour. A week later, it happened again, and again, enough times that my mother dragged me to get an MRI, convinced it was drug related. But, for once, I wasn't taking drugs. The doctors couldn't come up with a diagnosis. Looking back, my mysterious spasms surely had something to do with the stress of bouncing between school and clubland—burning the candle at both ends with a blowtorch.

Between my exhaustion and a merciless pollen allergy, which kicked up in the spring semester, I started missing classes. At one point, my dean summoned me to his office. I didn't mention the gigs, but I did accidentally sneeze all over his desk—a partial explanation, at least. One of the defiled papers was my Hebrew class attendance record. Alex and I had eagerly signed up at the start of the semester, proud Jewish boys determined to understand the language we'd recited at our Bar Mitzvahs with fuck-all idea what we were saying.

I made it to two classes. Alex, a better Jew and student than me, stuck with it. He called me up after the final exam to relay one of the questions:

קראמ הפיא?

[Where is Mark?]

* * *

Vinyl guru Ben Velez delivered on his promise to bring me into his coveted underground network of rare dealers. Our first stop: a record fair in the ballroom of the Roosevelt Hotel, on East Forty-Fifth Street. The hotel, built in the 1920s, was once so glamorous that Conrad Hilton lived in its presidential suite. Since then, the allure had faded, but its grand ballroom, with its ornate molding and glittering chandeliers, found new life hosting something far less fancy yet equally vital to New York's hip-hop culture: a monthly record convention. Dozens of dealers would line the room with tables, offering records impossible to find elsewhere. DJs, producers, and collectors eagerly scoured the crates and traded music that helped shape a genre. According to legend, this was the very ballroom where Large Professor gifted Pete Rock the Tom Scott album that Rock sampled for "They Reminisce over You (T.R.O.Y.)."

But such generosity was rare. Most guarded their finds like state secrets. Few shared their discoveries, fearing someone might sample them first. The paranoid spirit of pioneering DJ Kool Herc—known for scrubbing the labels off his records to guard his party-rocking breaks—was alive and well in the Roosevelt ballroom.

The top-tier dealers claimed corner booths, erecting makeshift cardboard walls adorned with their most tantalizing offerings. I walked in with one mission: to hunt down as many records as I could afford that had been sampled by A Tribe Called Quest. I'd memorized the credits to Tribe's latest masterpiece, *Midnight Marauders*, and committed the sampled tracks to memory—Cal Tjader, Black Heat, Freddie Hubbard, Gary Bartz. If I'd devoted half as much brain space to my textbooks as I did to hip-hop liner notes, I would've been on the dean's list instead of in the dean's office. But these were my priorities. Q-Tip, the group's producer and rapper, was a genius and a hero of mine.

First, I spotted a record by RAMP, the Roy Ayers Music Production. Ayers, a sixties post-bop jazz vibraphonist turned seventies jazz-funk mastermind, had become known for his tightly arranged slices of disco and soul full of polished session musicianship. But the RAMP record was different, sounding as if it had been recorded in a single day, a few musicians in a room channeling something raw and transcendent. The vocals weren't like the soaring hooks of hits like "Running Away." They were sweeter, softer—like two girls singing side by side on a swing set in summer.

Q-Tip had come upon RAMP in a Queens record store five years back and discovered the perfect loop for what would become "Bonita Applebum," A Tribe Called Quest's iconic love song. RAMP's "Daylight" featured a chord progression that danced between major and minor tonalities, creating a musical landscape that was simultaneously uplifting and melancholic, perfectly capturing the essence of young love—that mixture of hope and heartache. By looping these chords, Q-Tip translated this emotional complexity into hip-hop's most poignant love letter, and thereby turned this obscure Roy Ayers side project into a holy grail record. Unlike Michael Jackson's *Thriller* or Fleetwood Mac's *Rumours*, which had millions of copies floating around, modest sellers like RAMP were infinitely harder to come by. Only a few thousand copies of the album were pressed up when it came out. DJs wanted it to play it out. Producers wanted to comb through it for more samples. Collectors needed to own it. Q-Tip originally paid five bucks for it, but the record—once overlooked treasure—was now hip-hop history.

I stared at the price tag: one hundred dollars.

Not today.

I spent all day chasing Tribe samples. Their music was artful and gorgeous, as were the jazz and soul gems from which they stitched it together. I saw the Grant Green record with the moody slow-burn guitar groove, *Down Here on the Ground*, that gave "Vibes and Stuff" its "vibes." Price tag: one hundred dollars.

Weldon Irvine's "We Gettin' Down"? That's the electric piano that drives "Award Tour." Price tag: forty dollars. And Jimmy McGriff's "Green Dolphin Street," where Tip turned the first few seconds of a band finding their footing into "Jazz (We've Got)"? Price tag: fifty dollars. I also spotted Ronnie Foster's "Mystic Brew." A rare seventies fusion record on the Blue Note label, its unconventional three-bar progression broke every rule of hip-hop sampling. Rappers almost always rhymed over even numbers of bars, A-B, A-B—what can you do with only three lines? Tribe showed us on "Electric Relaxation." Price tag: eighty dollars.

I found Minnie Riperton's *Adventures in Paradise*. Two of its songs showed up in the Tribe canon. The bass line of "Baby, This Love I Have" anchors "Check the Rhime"; a passage from "Inside My Love," with its somber Fender Rhodes phrase and Minnie holding a whistle-register F6 long enough to give Maria Callas a run for her money, was what gave "Lyrics to Go" its haunting mood. Price tag: twenty dollars.

I picked up an album by Rotary Connection, a band that once featured Riperton as their lead singer. A second sample for "Bonita Applebum" came from the sitar on the track "Memory Band." I held up the LP.

"How much?" I asked.

"Twenty bucks," the dealer—an elegant older man with short dreads and thick-rimmed glasses—said, eyeing me over his frames. I handed over the cash and kept digging.

And then, as I was leaving, I saw Q-Tip.

I felt a rush of star-struck panic. Clutching the Rotary Connection record that he had sampled, I scrambled to think of something to say that would casually exhibit some kind of crate-digging camaraderie.

"Hey, this is the record you guys sampled for 'Bonita,' right?" I asked, trying to sound chill, like we were peers in any conceivable universe.

He glanced at me, shrugged, and said, "I don't know," before walking off. Legends were still guarding the samples that they'd already made famous. It was mercenary out here.

Next up, Ben took me to Fort Greene to meet his Japanese dealer, San. On the train, Ben coached me on traditional Japanese etiquette so I wouldn't embarrass him. "San will show the records when he's ready. Don't ask to see them before he offers." As if one false move might curse us both to a lifetime of subpar pressings.

San welcomed us into his place, a tidy apartment with a few plants and a mid-century Zen vibe. In his striped sailor shirt and mussed hair, he looked like an NYU film student studying French new wave. We took off our shoes at the door and sat cross-legged on the floor. He lit incense and brought us green tea.

Eventually, he led us to his back room. Cardboard boxes over-flowed with records so rare I had no clue what half of them were. *24-Carat Black* was an album that went for one hundred dollars a pop: San had an entire sealed box. I wondered what drove this quiet Japanese man who spoke no English and seemed oblivious to hip-hop to scour small American towns and abandoned press-ing plants, to bring gold to the rap producers who made up his clientele.

I headed back to Poughkeepsie—another train, another exhausted morning. It was December 1994. I was midway through my sopho-more year, but it was clear that I didn't want to be there anymore. I'd wrung everything I could from it. There was a strange comfort in the thought of staying—three more years wrapped in the cocoon of campus life, the elms, maples, and beech trees buffering the storms of adulthood for just a little bit longer. But it was time.

Driving home for Christmas break, I told my mother my plan to leave.

"You're not dropping out of college, though," she said sternly.

"No, of course not. I'll transfer somewhere in the city."

The car went quiet. To break the silence, I turned on the local

Hudson Valley classic rock station. After a few songs, Billy Squier's "The Stroke" came on.

I had a flash of déjà vu.

"Wasn't Billy Squier the first concert you took us to?"

"Yes," she answered, matter-of-factly. "He had a crush on me. Even made custom tour T-shirts for all you kids. One time after his show at Wemb—"

"Can we save this story for another time? Ideally when I've left this earthly plane?" The appalled teenager in me couldn't hold back.

"Fine," she said, fighting a smile as we headed south. I stared out the window, watching the Hudson blur past. A restless spirit leaving school for the pull of the big city—I was echoing the same move she'd pulled at my age, just twenty-five years ago.

She couldn't stop me. There was too much of her in me.

FIVE

IT'S A DJ'S NIGHTMARE.

Early in the night. No crowd, no dancers. Your hands are idle.

Then you spot a stranger heading right for you. You don't know who it is, but here they come, mind-numbing small talk on the tip of their tongue. You're clearly unoccupied, there's nowhere to hide, and now you're trapped with a starry-eyed idiot dying to let you know he went to your high school.

It is in precisely this manner that I finally came face-to-face with my hero, Stretch Armstrong. Guess who the idiot was.

SETTING

A dark nightclub on Bond Street, around 11:00 p.m. The empty dance floor reverberates with eighties R&B. In the booth, we find STRETCH ARMSTRONG, a tall, rail-thin DJ, leaning against the decks. He looks bored, glancing around the empty room.

MARK RONSON

Enter MARK, from stage left, wearing a PNB jacket that swamps his frame. He stops momentarily, staring at the DJ booth. His baby face radiates awe.

MARK
(to himself, barely a whisper)
This is it. Stretch Armstrong. My hero.

[MARK takes a deep breath and strides toward the booth. STRETCH, noticing him, furrows his brow in anticipatory irritation.]

MARK
(grinning wide, overly eager)
Hey! I'm Mark. I went to Collegiate. I DJ, too...
[STRETCH stiffens in disdain.]

STRETCH
Collegiate? Wow. That place sucked. Who brags
about that?
[MARK laughs nervously, scrambling to recover.]

MARK
Yeah—no, totally. So wack.
[STRETCH raises an eyebrow, unimpressed. MARK flails for common ground.]
Can you believe there were only three Black
students in my entire class?
[MARK pauses mid-sentence, realizing he's veered into dangerous territory, fumbling to land the thought.]

NIGHT PEOPLE

(*voice trailing*)

...but they were my good friends.

[CRASH! BOOM! CARNAGE! STRETCH stares in disbelief]

STRETCH

(*curtly*)

Okay...nice to meet you, man.

[STRETCH turns back to the decks without another word. MARK stands frozen, a deer in the headlights of his own humiliation. He retreats toward the edge of the stage, addressing the audience directly as a spotlight isolates him.]

MARK

(*to the audience, running a hand through his hair*)

What the fuck is wrong with me?! This compulsive need to impress people, saying dumb shit hoping to make them like me.

(*mocking himself, mimicking his earlier tone*)

"But they were my good friends." Really? What was that?!

[MARK lets out a heavy sigh and gestures toward the booth, where STRETCH remains a distant silhouette, focused on the mix.]

(*softly*)

It didn't matter that I made an ass out of myself.

Or that he wasn't exactly a beacon of warmth.

[The music swells slightly—a hard boom-bap DJ Premier beat. MARK's face brightens in admiration.]

MARK RONSON

(*to the audience*)

I stayed and watched his whole set. Every
record, every trick. He wasn't just *playing*
music; he was a master puppeteer—invisible
strings ran from his fingers to the entire
crowd. He dropped "DWYCK" and ducked the volume right on Guru's line "I wreck the mic like
a pimp pimps hoes"—and the whole crowd rapped
along as one. Then, on the word "hoes," the
fourth beat of the bar—

[MARK mimes a DJ scratching]

—he surprised them by dropping the bass line
from "Gin and Juice." I thought the walls were
gonna cave in.

[MARK takes a beat, his expression shifting to mischief and guilt.]

The cardinal rule of hip-hop says, "no biting." But I couldn't help myself—I had to
steal it. And I used it so much, I started to
believe it was mine.

[The music fades slightly as MARK steps back into the shadows. He
looks over his shoulder at the booth one last time.]

MARK

(*softly, to himself*)

It was perfect.

[MARK exits stage right. Lights fade to black. A faint hum of bass
shakes the stage as the curtain falls.]

* * *

I shadowed Stretch all over the city. He played a series of weekly parties at venues like Bond Street, the Grand, and Don Hill's. Most of these events were the work of a promoter duo who went by their first names, Bill and Carlos. Their newest venture, True, was held at the Manhattan Brewing Company, a converted Con Edison substation on Watts, a tiny traffic-jammed street that funneled drivers out of SoHo and into the Holland Tunnel to New Jersey.

The party captured everything Bill and Carlos did best. The flyer, designed by the graffiti artist and Def Jam art director Cey Adams, popped with swirly blue psychedelic letters—like a Fillmore poster reimagined for the hip-hop era—printed on glossy 4-by-5-inch calling cards that covered every trendy shop counter south of Union Square. Then there was the venue. Bill and Carlos never settled for the familiar; they hunted architectural oddities and raw industrial caverns. The Manhattan Brewing Company towered with forty-foot ceilings and massive brick walls lined with rusted steel girders, Stretch commanding the tall stage like a hip-hop overlord perched above a downtown cocktail of graffiti legends, hipsters, weed dealers, skate rats, streetwear designers, underground rappers, hardcore kids, and industry insiders.

It wasn't just a scene—it was the apex of downtown nightlife, a spiritual successor to the Roxy's legendary Friday nights back in the eighties, where Afrika Bambaataa and Blondie first bridged the Bronx-to-Bowery divide.

Downtown had a hierarchy of places where DJs wanted to play. On the lower tier, you had "model parties" such as the ones at Tabac and Flowers. These lounges attracted the pretty people and fashion set, but musically they were a step behind—playing tracks that had already rocked Bill and Carlos parties months earlier. On the second tier were the raw hip-hop spots like the Koop and Sunday Soul Lounge, where the music was on point but the crowds lacked some of the cultural cross-pollination. Above them all were Bill and Carlos. No one could match their scale or flavor. They had the coolest crowd, the boundary-pushing vision—and they had Stretch.

Bill Spector—aka "Bill"—was a Jewish rap fanatic from Queens who wore bookish glasses and self-deprecatingly referred to himself as "the hip-hop Woody Allen," embracing his jittery neuroses. There was something outwardly and unapologetically Jewish about Bill Spector that I admired. Growing up, our Jewish role models were limited to scholars and intellectuals—Einstein, Freud. But when it came to musicians, the pickings were slim. I remember hearing David Lee Roth supposedly trained to be a rabbi, and it made me like Van Halen that little bit more. And of course, all good Jewish boys worshipped the Beasties.

As I got older, I realized there were plenty of Jews in music—they just weren't onstage. They were A&Rs and execs, like Dante Ross, who signed De La Soul, and Lyor Cohen, who ran Def Jam. But Bill wasn't a label guy. He was a kid from Kew Gardens who seemed to wear the same white Hanes V-neck and cargo shorts every night, standing on one side of the velvet rope while three hundred clubgoers waited in line on the other side, growing angrier by the minute. And in a culture that wasn't totally foreign to antisemitism, that took a certain kind of nerve.

At fourteen, I fell in love with Public Enemy's *Fear of a Black Planet*. The combination of the Bomb Squad's production and

Chuck D's raps was dizzying and brilliant. But the album arrived in the wake of controversy. On May 22, 1989, Professor Griff claimed in the *Washington Times* that Jews were responsible for "the majority of wickedness that goes on across the globe." In the uproar, Chuck D was pressured to fire Griff and apologize. A fiery lyric on *Fear* seemed to disown the apology, implying coercion rather than any genuine remorse, and I felt the sting. Still, I couldn't stop myself from rapping along with Chuck's commanding baritone.

Listening to that album on repeat, guilt coursed through me, thinking of my mother's father, Fred, who fled Nazi-occupied Austria, or my grandfather Henry and uncle Gerald, who fought Nazi sympathizers in London. My heritage, my faith, and my sense of Jewishness ran deep. In shul on Yom Kippur, surrounded by hundreds of fellow Jews, all of us etched with centuries of persecution, I was overwhelmed by a sense of belonging. This wouldn't be the last time I found antisemitism in the music or public pronouncements of some of the artists I admired most. Still, I couldn't forgo the brilliance of the Bomb Squad's beats, and I kept listening, hooked. There would have been a willful ignorance to focusing on myself as a victim in a genre of music that had been forged by Black Americans living in circumstances of crushing injustice. Jews were a part of white America; some of the record executives who had stolen publishing rights from artists in the early days were Jewish. This didn't make antisemitic lyrics or sentiments defensible, but it put things in perspective. If there were moments in which I was despised for who I was born as, it also attuned me, in some small way, to the vast suffering outside of my own circumstances.

It's also true that, in the downtown music scene, I felt very little tension between Black people and Jewish people. Jewish DJs played for Black promoters, Black DJs played for Jewish promoters, and we all hung tough. Still, I was drawn to Bill. For every sentence that ended with a Seinfeldian upward pitch and accompanying shoulder shrug, I liked him more and more.

By the time I met Bill, he was already a downtown legend. Clued-up Vassar kids spoke of him and Sheets and Pillows, an early-nineties party that he put on, with wide eyes. Featuring Stretch—still known as DJ Adrian B back then—the weekly Friday jam drew massive crowds and gave acts like Del tha Funkee Homosapien and Cypress Hill their New York debuts.

The party hopped venues weekly, always one step ahead of panicked owners who heard the phrase "hip-hop" and immediately pictured their bar razed to the ground. Bill, ever the salesman, would assure them with a straight face, "We play house music." Then the drums of Schoolly D's "P.S.K. What Does It Mean?" would hit, and all hell would break loose. Owners sprinted around in meltdown mode, demanding Bill change the music or shut it down. But with a line snaking around the block, all they could do was pace nervously, muttering prayers the night wouldn't end in violence.

Often, it did, when rival crews squared off, turning the dance floor into a scene from *Roadhouse*.

Money was rolling in, but the chaos of dealing with club owners, cops, and weekly melees wore Bill down. After one violent night too many, he pulled the plug on Sheets and Pillows. At twenty-five, he was ulcer ridden, exhausted, and done with promoting—or so he thought. Then Carlos showed up.

Carlos was a magnetic, twenty-two-year-old Dominican from uptown who'd lived for Sheets and Pillows. For him, it wasn't just a party, it was a highlight of his youth. Determined to resurrect it, he tracked Bill down at his day job and wouldn't take no for an answer. Bill relented and the two joined up. There was something about this odd duo of uptown charm and downtown hustle that struck nightlife gold. Bond Street and a string of incredible parties were born.

I hung around Bill at his parties, bugging him to let me open. "Yeah, kid. When you're ready," he'd say, in a way that managed to be both warm and dismissive. Bill's DJs were heavyweights: Clark Kent, Stretch Armstrong, and Mighty Mi. Clark, who hailed from Brooklyn, was considered by many—including Stretch—to be the greatest club DJ in New York. Stretch was *the* downtown DJ. Even the new guy on the scene, Mighty Mi, had spent five or six years building his name in Boston.

Bill was probably right to shut me down. I was barely a year into the game, and already eyeing the throne. But after feeling that crown, the energy of a Bill and Carlos party, I was possessed. I kept cranking out demo mixtapes to showcase what I could do. And I made damned sure to have one in my pocket every time I went out. Just in case.

Six months after my brush-off from Bill, a friend introduced me to Carlos on the dance floor at Soul Kitchen. "I come to all your parties," I said, overexcited. "They're the best. I'd love to play sometime. Here's a demo tape." I handed it to him.

Carlos flashed a grin. "Thanks."

Two days later, he called.

"I've got a slot for you Friday at Tilt—our new party Nut n' Honey. Stretch is downstairs. You'll play upstairs, opening for DJ Jules."

"Wow. You won't regret this. And thanks for listening to the tape!"

"What tape?" he said. "Oh. I didn't listen to your tape...Be there at ten." *Click.*

I stood there, holding the phone.

I was in.

I got right to work, practicing for Friday. I was living back with my mother and stepfather in their rental, a new high-rise at Eighty-Eighth Street and Central Park. My mother had traded down her fancy Majorelle and deco furniture for white linen couches against plain white walls. My bedroom in the last place had been a trust-fund fever dream—an electronic drum kit, neon lighting, even a stage truss with spotlights. My new bedroom was simpler—four walls, a gray metal bunk bed, and a desk housing my turntables. What else did I need?

Opening for Jules would mean one thing—*no hits.* That's the opener's golden rule: Warm the crowd up, set the tone, and leave the glory to the headliner. If they dig how you play, maybe you'll get invited back. This meant leaving the bangers at home. Instead of Gang Starr's "Mass Appeal," I'd play "Code of the Streets." Smif-N-Wessun's "Bucktown" got shelved for "Sound Bwoy Bureill." Ill Al Skratch's "Where My Homiez?" was swapped out for "Get Dough." My set would be B-sides, underground joints, R&B sleepers, and classics—basically DJ foreplay.

Friday afternoon, I made my way to Rock and Soul—the record store run by an Israeli woman and her daughters that was at the heart of the city's hip-hop scene. Fridays were always a madhouse, with DJs frantically stocking up for their weekend gigs. Shirley Bechor, the store's formidable matriarch, commanded the chaos with a pricing gun in hand, swatting away the restless crowd like flies. "Wait until I label it!" she would say sharply. I picked up Nas's

"The World Is Yours," O.C.'s "Time's Up," and a few R&B records before heading home, my arsenal now complete.

*   *   *

Tilt was on Varick Street in a no-man's-land south of the West Village and west of SoHo. In the daytime, the neighborhood's high-rise office towers and delis bustled with activity, but at night, it emptied out—except for the clubs: Manhattan Brewing Company, S.O.B.'s, Buddha Bar.

Security out front looked like the starting defensive line of a football team as styled by the Black Panthers. I dragged two crates and a record bag up the stairs and into a room the size of a high school gymnasium, with polished-wood parquet floors to match. A projector threw up *Wild Style*–era photos of young b-boys in Kangol hats and graffiti artists bombing beat-up subway cars. A bar lined one side, while a stage on the other hosted a rap group mid–sound check. The DJ onstage was trying to scratch a phrase from a song by Nice & Smooth, but it kept skipping. He hopped offstage and walked over to me.

It was DJ On-E. Only eighteen months earlier, I'd stood in awe, watching him spin on that revelatory night at the Shelter. And now, here I was, playing under the same roof as him—and Stretch, and Jules.

"Yo, you got a copy of Nice & Smooth's 'Funky for You' I can borrow?"

"Sure…I used to come see you at NASA, man," I said, underplaying it for a change.

Handing someone a record to use in their scratch routine is like handing your car keys to a stuntman and saying, "Just don't hit *all* the walls." I gave it to him anyway.

When the doors opened, I took over, but, after an hour, the vibe wasn't clicking. The room was less than half-full with about fifty people—some rolling blunts in the corner, others hovering near the floor. I darted up and down the stairs constantly to hear what the main-floor DJ was spinning. If I heard R&B, I played reggae. If I heard reggae, I switched to classics. I tried to crack the code. Nothing stuck.

DJ Jules finally rolled in, pushing two crates of records balanced on a skateboard. He looked like he'd come straight from Basquiat's apartment circa 1985: tilted Kangol, Adidas shell-toes. As he unpacked, I spotted a Faze-O record front and center.

"That's a dope record," I said, hoping to start a conversation.

"I might have an extra at home, mate," he said in an English accent that reminded me of the scruffy, skinny guys behind the counters of London's Soho record shops.

Like many of them, Jules was a "soul boy"—heir to a British subculture that emerged after World War II, born when American Forces Network and Radio Luxembourg introduced British ears to jazz, blues, and R&B. In the sixties, while the BBC droned on with stuffy in-house orchestras, my dad and his generation tuned into the Radio Caroline "pirate" radio station broadcasting illegally from ships in international waters. He'd hear Booker T. & the M.G.'s and race to the record store Friday with a hundred other teens, all desperate for a copy.

Twenty years younger, Jules carried that torch as part of the "rare groove" generation. Instead of hunting Otis Redding, he searched for forgotten seventies gems by underappreciated American artists like Donald Byrd, Roy Ayers, and Lonnie Liston Smith, masters of deep grooves, jazzy chords, and lush strings. Different decades, same obsession.

I stuck close to Jules all night, fetching drinks like a dutiful apprentice. Something about him struck a chord, like finding a piece of myself I'd misplaced. Having spent half my life caught between London and New York, I was never sure if I felt English, American, or some strange hybrid of both. Being around Jules—this Londoner transplanted to Manhattan who'd managed to keep his identity intact—felt comforting.

I wandered downstairs to watch Stretch, who had the room jam-packed. He dropped the syrupy R. Kelly slow jam "Your Body's Callin'," and I wondered if he was fucking with the crowd. Eight bars in, he blended in the instrumental of Jeru the Damaja's "Come Clean"—a DJ Premier beat as raw as a 3:00 a.m. back-alley brawl in East New York. It was a little tongue-in-cheek, and, most important, it sounded phenomenal. I'd be stealing it soon enough. Who knows why I thought it was okay to pilfer those mixes. Maybe I convinced myself it was a kind of tribute. If I could've held up a big sign that said THIS MIX BELONGS TO STRETCH ARMSTRONG while doing it, I would have. It wasn't about the credit. It just sounded too good not to use it. I couldn't help myself.

The next Friday at Tilt was better than the first, and Jules came through with the extra copy of Faze-O. One of the security guys brought a tiny TV with a rabbit-ear antenna so we could all catch the Knicks game outside. The Knicks were in the '94 NBA Finals, uniting the city in a frenzy that made you hug anyone in even a hint of orange and blue. Between records, I'd run downstairs to watch a few minutes of action, then dash back upstairs to change the track.

On the way up, a posse of Upper East Side girls in headbands and pearls who didn't resemble the regular clientele gathered by the stairs. Carlos pointed out an underage blonde with exceptionally well-ironed hair.

"Who the fuck is that?" he asked.

"Trump's daughter," Bill said with a shrug.

A wild and bloody brawl broke out at True the next week, getting Bill and Carlos booted from the Manhattan Brewing Company. They moved their flagship Saturday party to Tilt but couldn't sustain both nights at the same venue. Friday—my night—became the casualty.

And with that, my brief brush with the upper echelon of the downtown scene evaporated. And what did I have to show for it? A few weeks playing to a half-empty room where I couldn't even fill the dance floor, let alone impress anyone who mattered.

I'd done nothing to change Bill's impression that I was too green. The brutal truth sank in: This might be the closest I was going to get to the scene. To make matters worse, my friend got into a fistfight with one of Bill's buddies from Queens on the last night.

The death blow came when I heard Stretch had found out I was biting his mixes.

I might as well go back to Poughkeepsie.

* * *

After getting iced out by the top-tier players, I was hustling for second- and third-tier gigs wherever I could find them. College parties, uptown bars, anything that covered cab fare and the week's haul of new records. Most of what I made went right into the hands of record stores and private dealers. With street vendors everywhere, each walk through the Village or SoHo became a financial gauntlet—any corner a potential money pit. I'd drop to my knees on the grimy sidewalk, rifling through stacks on Sixth Avenue as pedestrians brushed past, my digging sessions soundtracked by the grunts and cheers of the West Fourth Street basketball courts.

The Chelsea flea market on Twenty-Fifth Street was a gold mine for digging records. Dozens upon dozens of vendors set up their tables across the area, selling everything from moth-eaten Levis and Art Deco lamps to water-damaged *Playboys* and sepia family photos from the Depression. Between this ancient Americana, I unearthed my own treasures: twelve-inch singles by T. S. Monk, Rick James, and the real prize—a copy of Chic's "Le Freak" stamped with a curious mark: "BPI—Black Passions Incorporated," a DJ's homemade logo.

New, sealed records were pristine and perfect, but they were products. A used record that had lived in a DJ's crate had soul. The BPI DJ, whoever he or she was, had probably bought the record when it dropped in '78. I imagined playing "Le Freak" to a crowd for the very first time—before it was an all-time classic, when it was just the new Chic joint.

This disc was a time capsule of sweat-soaked clubs and dancers I'd never know. And now, I was the newest link in a chain that might stretch across decades of dance floors to come. Would some future DJ one day hold this same record and wonder about me?

Digging gave new purpose to summer trips to London to visit my father. I spent days loitering in the record shops of Berwick Street. The clerks smoked rollies while exuding a jaded profundity that made me feel unqualified to exist in their presence.

I discovered *Classic Jazz-Funk Mastercuts*, a double-disc compilation packed with rare gems that were spun at Soul Kitchen. A Roy

Ayers greatest hits comp had four or five Soul Kitchen standards that would've run me two hundred dollars. For twenty pounds, it was a steal. Even better were the true rarities—UK-only pressings of the Brand New Heavies, a group of rare-groove revivalists whose debut album was a favorite.

At this point, I was out of cash so I walked into a tomato-red phone booth on the corner of Tottenham Court Road, fed twenty pence into the slot, and asked the operator to connect me to the offices of Acid Jazz Records—the band's label.

"Hi, my name's Mark Ronson. I'm a very important club DJ from New York. I'm in town and might have some time to pick up a few promos."

There was a pause. Then, with the unsure tone of someone who couldn't decide if I was the next Grandmaster Flash or a child running a scam, he replied, "Yeah, sure. We have some stuff here."

"Good," I said. "I'll be by in fifteen minutes."

The rest of the week, I spent at my father's office, a small VHS-distribution company tucked above Marylebone High Street. He'd turned his life around and married my stepmother, Michelle, a successful fashion model whose own life had been far from a picnic. Born in London to an American father and Irish Indian mother who split up when she was young, Michelle spent ages four to sixteen being sent off to a series of convents and parochial schools. The string of stepmothers her father brought into her life treated her so horribly that she vowed to never do that to anyone else. She loved me and my sisters as her own, even bringing us on her honeymoon with my dad. Together, they had three children: my sister Henrietta and my brothers David and Josh.

After losing his old business, my father started from scratch. Sharp and entrepreneurial, with a love of movies, he came up with a business plan: acquire the rights to B movies, repackage them with slick new artwork, and sell them to high-street shops like Woolworths and WHSmith—cheap enough to undercut the A-list titles. He'd recently acquired the rights to a pile of kung fu films, and my job that week was to clean up the clunky language in the subtitles.

He had a stereo in his office with a tape deck, so I popped in a mixtape I'd been working on. He leaned against the doorway, cigarette in one hand, listening to a blend of Apache's "Gangsta Bitch" into Madonna's "Erotica." As the drumbeats fused, a small smile spread across his face.

"This is really good," he said, a mixture of surprise and pride.

The affirmation resonated in my bones. He was the one who planted this fixation with rhythm, beats, and groove inside me. Not even an ocean between us could break that connection. He still kept his old vinyl in the office, loads of funk and soul—Prince, James Brown, Boz Scaggs. I started flipping through them. "You should let me take these back to New York and sell them for you," I said, knowing full well they would be going straight into my own crates.

"All right," he said, although something told me he understood exactly what I intended.

He sent me back to New York with two boxes of classics. Whatever was inside, they were worth infinitely more than anything I could've found on Berwick Street.

SIX

R^{ING.}

*R*ING.

The muffled chirp of the Sony cordless echoed from somewhere in the room, sounding like an eight-bit baby bird that had fallen from its nest. But where was it? Under a pillow? In the pocket of a hoodie? Inside last night's pizza box?

I glanced at my roommate, Jason, sprawled on the other couch, his thumbs twitching on the PlayStation controller the only sign of life. Jason was a top male model and it-boy of the downtown fashion scene whom I'd met at Café Tabac. I had the apartment lined up and needed a roommate quickly.

I'd moved out of my parents' house and into this two-bedroom apartment in Murray Hill—a midtown neighborhood filled with young families pushing babies and old people pushing laundry—Manhattan's multigenerational conveyor belt. There were no trendy nightspots—just reliable delis, local restaurants, and dive bars serving residents and NYU Medical staff. We lived down the street from a row of South Asian restaurants that earned our hood the nickname

"Curry Hill." Leaving for a gig, I'd always smell cumin and coriander wafting down the block, yellow-cab drivers double-parked out front eating kebab and biryani.

There was nothing cool about the neighborhood or the apartment, a 1970s build with parquet floors and windows framed in tarnished brass. But I didn't care. It was mine. Our only decoration was a TV and the two white couches on which we were now both stretched out.

"Jason," I said. "You got the phone?"

"Nah," he muttered, eyes glued to the screen.

Ring.

I scanned the room, then shoved my hand between the cushions, pulling out two cigarette butts, one Nike sock, and a couple of headphone adapters.

Ring.

The answering machine clicked on. A clipped, gravelly voice cut through the room: "Hi, this is Evan from Buddha Bar, looking for Mark Ronson. I need a DJ tonight…"

Buddha Bar?!

I had ten seconds before this guy hung up and moved on, and it was the only decent job offer I'd had in months.

The voice continued, "Get back to me ASAP at…"

I dropped to my knees, thrusting my arm under the couch until my fingers brushed plastic. Found it! But the phone was wedged stuck. All I could do was hit talk.

"Yes, this is he!" I shouted into the void beneath the couch.

"I need a DJ tonight. Eleven to four. You free?"

Hell, yes. An end to my banishment from downtown.

"Of course!" I said. "Uh…how much?" As if I wouldn't have done it for cab fare and three drink tickets.

"Two hundred."

"See you tonight."

I hung up, still sprawled on the floor. The squalor of the living room stretched before me: overflowing ashtrays, half-eaten mozzarella sticks in greasy takeout boxes, and records scattered everywhere. Our galley kitchenette was somewhere we ventured only to throw out the trash—when we remembered. It always oozed green sludge by the time I took it out, even though almost nothing that went in it was green. But I spent so little time at home, it barely mattered. The apartment was just a crash pad—somewhere to sleep and practice before heading out to work.

Making good on my promise to my mother, I had enrolled as an undergraduate at NYU. But I hadn't even considered living in the dorms. I was back in the city to DJ while going to college, not the other way around. Rent was covered by a one-thousand-dollar monthly stipend from a trust fund my grandfather had set up before he died. Most of the money had been earmarked for my schooling. Some of it had been spectacularly blown on a Bar Mitzvah at Tavern on the Green, a crystal palace of a restaurant in Central Park with chandeliers, hundreds of mirrors, and as many white-gloved waiters. Money that I could have been spending on rare breaks was instead partly squandered on Bar Mitzvah performers such as a breakdancer dressed as Mozart, spinning on his head while lip-syncing Falco's novelty hit "Rock Me Amadeus."

Thanks to my departed grandfather, as long as I booked two gigs a week, I could keep things afloat. But ever since Tilt, the gigs had been humbling—after-work parties, random uptown bars, whatever helped out.

I still enjoyed myself in the moment, even if the crowds were bland. Validation is validation, even in a pair of Dockers. But it wasn't downtown.

Buddha Bar, on the other hand! I'd heard its name so many times: "Have you been to Buddha?" "We're going to Buddha Bar tonight." "Did you hear what happened at Buddha Bar last Sunday?" The alliteration amplified its romance and mystery. From what I knew, it attracted a clientele similar to Café Tabac's, though Tabac was more of a velvet-roped realm where the fashion set played pool and smoked a lot of cigarettes. Buddha Bar, on the other hand, had a dance floor and drew serious DJs like Jules and Stretch. Sunday nights were home to Juicy, a white-hot party thrown by DJ Belinda and Lysa Cooper.

Belinda Becker was a downtown fixture. One night, when she was busing tables at Area, word spread that a DJ had no-showed. The panicked manager yelled, "Does anyone know music?!" She did. Within a week, she was spinning in the back lounge, launching her career. Lysa was her close friend, an in-demand stylist, DJ, and trendsetter, raised in the Bronx, five foot ten with a magnificent blown-out 'fro who channeled seventies glamour through fabric she'd cut and sewn herself.

Belinda and Lysa referred to Juicy as a "women's strip club," with strict entry rules—men could only enter accompanied by three women—in the firm belief that parties were better with fewer men around. I tried to go, but by the time I got to calling a third female friend, someone would catch on: "Mark, we're not going to be your fucking plus-three so you can get into Juicy tonight."

Most nights, unless you were a supermodel, knew supermodels, or were related to one, you weren't getting in. The exception seemed to be Lenny Kravitz. When he walked into a room, supermodels materialized out of thin air. That didn't stop my friend Simon Rex and me from wasting our nights outside, declaring, "We're with Lenny. He must have forgot to put us on the list."

Buddha Bar's cold-shoulder door policy reminded me of the uptown Prada store, where the salespeople seemed trained to treat you like dirt, knowing it made you desperate to spend. An eastern European saleswoman once watched me enter the store with such disdain that I instantly spent two entire weeks' worth of gig money on a dress for my mother's birthday, whipping out my Discover card to show *her* who was boss.

Rejection and denial—New York's most renewable resource. Even a Times Square Applebee's was drenched in attitude. I once flew to Indiana to visit a friend, and a pollen allergy overwhelmed me the moment we landed. I stopped at a gas station and asked if they had any Benadryl. "Sorry, we don't," the cashier said in a Midwestern drawl. "But I might have some Claritin out back in my truck."

My first thought was "ax murderer." But there was no catch. He just tossed me a blister pack of pills from the glove box. I remember nearly being moved to tears. And yet would I have lived there? God, no. Experiencing that level of kindness daily would have short-circuited me. I was far more at home standing outside some overhyped fortress of cool, where the doorman could size me up and decide I didn't have the right look.

But not tonight. Tonight I was getting in.

There was one real problem. I already had a gig at the not-so-cool Reminisce Lounge, a bar on the Upper East Side. Marcus Lin-ial, the owner, hired me after catching me downtown, wanting to bring some flavor to his patch of East Seventy-Third Street. In his late twenties, with puppy-dog eyes and a single gold stud, Marcus was from the suburb of New Rochelle and, at the right angle, bore a passing resemblance to George Michael. A singer who had once been signed to Clive Davis's J Records, Marcus had gotten close to pop stardom, but if he had any dashed dreams, he carried them lightly, though I could tell his heart was still in music. The animated way he'd talk about a video he'd discovered on BET suggested I was more than just his Friday DJ, but a kindred musical spirit amid this nondescript pocket of the city.

The Reminisce Lounge crowd wasn't hip. They didn't dress in Triple 5 Soul and Phat Farm—they came straight from work, in office casual from Filene's Basement. But they danced to the same shit people danced to downtown, and I'm sure they needed to let off steam as much as anyone else. I felt something honorable in playing for the working stiffs. What was a gigging bar DJ, if not Billy Joel's "Piano Man" in Air Max 90s—minus the harmonica and the tip jar.

I liked Marcus and was grateful for the check. But Buddha Bar, well, that was ten rungs up the ladder. There was no way I was schlepping uptown tonight, not after this opportunity had come my way.

I picked up the phone to call Marcus and his machine answered. A small victory out of the gate.

"[Cough, cough] Hey Marcus . . . feeling really under the weather tonight [cough]. Definitely coming down with something, so I won't be in. Don't worry, I've lined up someone great to fill in [more coughing]. Okay, see you next week."

I didn't love lying, but when it came to the club hustle and climbing the ladder, I was probably more cutthroat than I cared to say out loud. Still, if I found a replacement, what was the harm?

I called my boy Max Glazer, a great DJ who worked at Eightball Records—a small store on East Ninth Street specializing in dance music. The staff were all DJs, and intensely serious. Everyone who worked there terrified me. Except Max. Although he grew up in Woodstock, we shared a familiar trajectory, coming up as fans of Stretch Armstrong's radio show and sneaking into clubs as teenagers to catch his sets. Now we moved in similar circles, playing the same venues on different nights. He had held down Tuesdays at Café Tabac with Eli Escobar, another solid DJ my age, back when Ethan and I did Mondays.

Max was also a good dude, friendly and easygoing—something I couldn't say about everyone. The DJ scene had more than its share of haters, especially with thirty DJs vying for the same gigs. Some people resented me for coming from money. Others rolled their eyes when girls thought I was cute. Even with my career hitting a rough patch, my climb had been quick enough to rub people the wrong way.

"Hey, man," I said when he picked up, and then I gave him the rundown.

"I'm busy tonight," he replied, "but you could try Cosmo. Pretty sure he's free."

"Cosmo from Eightball?"

"Yeah, hit him up."

I hung up and hesitated. It was dicey bringing in someone I didn't know to cover for me with so much on the line, but I didn't have a choice.

I dialed Cosmo and told him the deal. He sounded reliable enough, though a faint indifference colored his voice. But hearing the scratch of pencil on paper as he jotted the address set my mind at ease some.

I hung up. Crisis averted. Time to get ready.

Kneeling on the parquet floor of our cramped entryway, I sorted my records for the night. I had now amassed a few hundred, and they were everywhere: crammed into plastic milk crates, leaning against walls, and stacked like Jenga towers. First-time visitors always froze in the doorway, their faces flickering between panic and disbelief as they navigated my vinyl minefield.

My crates stayed in the entryway because, after a gig, I barely had the strength to lug them from the cab to the elevator. Carrying them the extra four feet to my bedroom was out of the question. Still, taking those same exact records to the next gig was equally unthinkable. Part of the ritual—part of the work—was pulling them apart, flipping through each crate to mentally rehearse the night ahead.

Album covers provided visual cues that helped me start building up a set. The lipstick-red telephone on the cover of Kleeer's *Intimate Connection* instantly conjured the sharp, electro sounds of the Roland 808 drum machine in the songs' production. That 808 color led me to Marvin Gaye's "Sexual Healing," with its iconic rhythm track, then to Loose Ends' "Hangin' on a String" and

Chaka Khan's "Ain't Nobody." The Khan record wasn't made with a drum machine, but its moody synth lines made it a natural fit. And from "Ain't Nobody," a DJ could go anywhere—no dance floor could resist belting that "oh, oh, oh, oh" before the chorus. If you ducked the volume and let them sing it, that moment was a perfect pivot to drop anything from Soul II Soul to Souls of Mischief.

Sonic fragments—an 808 conga or an arpeggiated synth motif—hummed constantly in my brain. It was like I had a tiny antenna that was always alert for the frequency of music. Standing in line at the dry cleaner, I'd hear Bill Withers's "Lovely Day" and immediately think, That would go perfectly with "You Gonna Make Me Love Somebody Else," by the Jones Girls, pre-performing the blend in my brain. It's hard to stay present when your mind is constantly pairing tempos and keys instead of focusing on the person in front of you. But there was no off switch—short of a lobotomy.

I filled three milk crates and a Technics bag with the essentials: Barrington Levy, the Fatback Band, Bobby Konders, Gwen McCrae. These records, along with a few hundred others, made up New York's club canon: tracks that earned their status through Black radio play or as favorites of DJs like Kool Herc, Red Alert, and Frankie Inglese.

Learning the repertoire and then actually tracking down the records took relentless work. I discovered them by watching dozens of DJs, and by hanging out at stores like Rock and Soul long enough that an older DJ would see me pulling Fonda Rae's "Over Like a Fat Rat" and say, "If you like that, you need this," passing me Meli'sa Morgan's "Fool's Paradise." That's how we built our knowledge—through nights out and the kindness of our peers.

The downtown canon was a real thing. Seventy-five percent of our crates held the same discs. On any given night, you could dig through Mighty Mi's, Jules's, or Belinda's crates and find "Before I Let Go," by Maze Featuring Frankie Beverly, or "Genius of Love," by Tom Tom Club. The other 25 percent—the records that added an extra layer of personality—defined our style. I hadn't found mine yet. I was still catching up on the basics.

Finally, beyond the selections themselves, a downtown DJ set had a specific arc to it—a timetable. It wasn't documented, but it might as well have been nailed to the wall of every club like Martin Luther's theses—that's how well we knew it.

> **10:00 p.m.–12:00 a.m.: Soul & Disco Classics**
> **12:00–1:00 a.m.: Old-School Hip-Hop**
> **1:00–2:00 a.m.: New Hip-Hop & R&B**
> **2:00–2:30 a.m.: Dancehall**
> **2:30–3:00 a.m.: Hip-Hop**
> **3:00–4:00 a.m: Whatever It Takes To Keep 'Em**

It was a playbook we knew from watching those who came before us. Some put their own spin on it, but few fully veered off.

Time to get going. One last base to cover.

"Hey, Jason…"

He hit pause on the PlayStation and turned to me.

"I got an offer to play Buddha Bar tonight. It's a big opportunity, so I called Reminisce and told them I'm sick. If Marcus calls, just back me up—say I'm out cold in bed."

"I got you, bro."

Back when I was playing Tilt, I had no shortage of friends

willing to help me haul my crates to the club. It was a win-win for all involved: I got some extra muscle, and they got to skip the line, score some drink tickets, and hang in the booth. But nobody cared to tag along to Reminisce Lounge.

Whenever I'm on my own carting crates I'm reminded of that puzzle they ask you in school—the one with the farmer, the chicken, the bag of grain, and the fox. He has to get them all across the river without the fox killing the chicken or the chicken eating the grain.

This is the remix.

Mark's Challenge:

Mark has three crates of vinyl records, each weighing around sixty pounds, that need to be moved from his apartment to the elevator. He can only carry one crate at a time, and the journey involves keeping both the apartment door and the elevator door open. If the apartment door closes, it will lock him out, leaving the remaining crates stranded. If the elevator door closes, the elevator will leave, and Mark will have to summon it again—hoping that his prized possessions aren't swiped by another tenant.

Solution:

Mark hoists the first crate and carries it to the apartment door, wedging it in the doorway to keep it ajar. He returns to the apartment, lifts the second crate—which oddly feels heavier, though he knows it isn't—and carries it to the elevator, using it to prop the elevator door open. Back in the apartment, Mark braces himself for the third crate, lifts, grunts, and shuffles it to the elevator, setting it down inside. He returns to the apartment door, retrieves the first crate, and carries it to the elevator. Now, for the final act: a precise kick to the crate propping the elevator door open. If his aim is true, it will slide inside the elevator. If not, his lumbar will pay the price. With all three crates secured in the elevator, Mark presses "Lobby," catching his breath and trying not to think about the fact that he's about to have to repeat this process in reverse. And into a taxi.

* * *

Once in the cab, we headed down Lexington Avenue and a cooling breeze came through the cracked window. It was a perfect New York summer dusk, blue fading into black like a Rothko painting. We cut west on Fourteenth Street, south on Seventh Avenue, then rolled to a stop at the corner of Varick and Vandam, just a block away from Tilt's shuttered remains. I stepped out, gripping the first crate with both hands.

With a shove of my shoulder, the thick double doors swung open. A seductive red glow washed over me. Lighting is the unsung hero of New York nightlife. Recalling an epic night out, we often talk about the people who made things happen—musicians, DJs, the bathroom coke dealer—and the spaces themselves—warehouses, former power plants, deconsecrated churches. But rarely do you hear someone say, "This club is the shit! Who programmed the DMX setup? The fixture placement is super on point, too!" Whoever handled Buddha Bar earned their money.

The décor was minimal but chic: A mirrored bar ran the length of the right wall, its surface catching the crimson ambience. A small dance floor anchored the room, ringed by low wooden tables.

But hold up . . . what the fuck?!

There was already a DJ here. A Black dude in a flat wool cap, already set up and spinning like this was *his* gig. I hadn't just hauled 180 pounds of vinyl and risked getting fired from Reminisce to find out I'd been double-booked.

I walked over.

"Hi, I'm Mark. I'm supposed to be DJing tonight," I said, keeping it as polite as I could.

"Nope. I'm Jeff Brown, and I was booked to play tonight," he said, turning briefly from his blend. "Who the fuck are you?" Then he went right back to cueing his next record, as if I weren't the only person on the empty dance floor.

"Oh," I replied, trying a reset. "Maybe there's been a mistake. I'm sure there's a solu—"

"Man, you know what?!" he said, slamming his headphones down onto the mixer. "I'm sick of all you white boy DJs coming around and taking all the fucking gigs. This is bullshit, man. I'm done with it!"

The force of his words hit hard. Mainly because he was completely right. Downtown was flooded with white DJs spinning Black music. Everyone knew it.

No one questioned the credibility of Stretch Armstrong. He hosted the most influential underground radio show on the East Coast, and had helped break Wu-Tang, Jay-Z, and Fat Joe. But the scene itself was anything but even. The clubs, while diverse on the dance floor, were all in white neighborhoods and run by white owners. Some felt more comfortable around white DJs and gave them preferential treatment. A few were straight-up racist. Your average white DJ had too many things working in their favor. Myself included.

This music was created by Black people, for Black people. White DJs like me could spin it, love it, and even contribute, but what happened when we started taking gigs that should've gone to Black DJs?

I had no comeback. Plus, this whole thing felt like karma for lying to Marcus.

On the other hand, I really wanted this fucking gig. So I stepped back up to Jeff and gave it another shot.

"I'm sure there's some kind of deal where we can both play and still get paid. Would you mind if I talked to the manager for both of us?"

He gave me half a shrug.

After some back-and-forth, we worked it out to share the night. Split the time, split the pay. And a couple of songs into our shaky start, he saw I knew my shit and slowly began to thaw.

I liked him, too. He was prickly, with a sharp tongue and good taste.

As the place filled up, our back-and-forth was clicking. I took a gulp of my third Absolut and cranberry and caught a silhouette barreling through the doors.

This can't be happening.

But it was.

Marcus from Reminisce Lounge was striding purposefully through the crowd, looking furious, with a woman by his side. Maybe he's just on a really weird date, I thought, praying.

He scanned the room until his gaze landed on the booth. My chest tightened as he marched toward me.

"What the fuck is going on here?" he said. The question was clearly rhetorical.

"I, uh, well...I got this call...er, I was going to call you, but... it's, uh, because..." I sounded like I'd suddenly forgotten how sentences worked. But for the second time that night, I had nothing to say. I was so in the wrong, the only move was to shut up.

"You stood me up tonight," he said.

"What happened to Cosmo, though?" I blurted.

"Who the fuck is Cosmo?"

Jesus. Cosmo had bailed. Disastrous. The sequence of events was starting to come together in my head, Keyser Söze style: the Friday night crowd jammed shoulder to shoulder, Marcus glancing at his watch, his face changing from stressed concern to frantic desperation, juggling the bar while constantly running back and forth from the booth to change music that wasn't moving people, at least not in the way a DJ could.

But one thing didn't make sense: *How did Marcus know I was at Buddha Bar?* This wasn't the moment to ask.

"You know what?" Marcus said, his voice cold now. "Don't come back to work."

He turned, grabbed his date's hand, and stormed out the door.

The entire club seemed enveloped in fog. Lauryn Hill was playing, but her voice was muffled and distant. I liked Marcus. He'd looked out for me, trusted me, and I'd abandoned him. I was already struggling for work—and now I'd lost one of the few things I had going for me. I wondered if Jeff was enjoying this. But instead, he gave me a sympathetic shrug, his focus locked on the turntables, keeping the crowd moving. A few minutes later, he handed me the headphones—DJ 101 for "you got next." The crowd got into it, and my mood lifted. Their energy was feeding my ego, and the

Absolut-cranberry was feeding something else. Soon, I was feeling pretty damn good again. Jeff and I were trading tracks and laughs, all tension a thing of the past.

Then, at 4:00 a.m., the lights came on, deflating Buddha Bar's sexiness with harsh fluorescents that exposed every scuffed floorboard and dingy corner. I packed my records, exchanged numbers with Jeff, and headed out.

On the bumpy ride home, I thought about the mess I'd made. The vodka and validation had felt good, but it had hardly been worth the emotional fallout. I'd had some lucky breaks when I was starting out, but for the most part, there were no magical leaps forward in the grind of DJing. Your rep was as good as the people who vouched for it. You showed up, played well, and tried not to burn any bridges. I was stupid to think one night at Buddha Bar would change much. Tonight was just like any other night: heading home depleted, alone, and a little too tipsy.

Dragging my crates through the front door, I found Jason where I'd left him.

"Hey, man, how was your night?" I asked, setting my crates down.

"Chill. Some dope new games I picked up."

"Cool. Did anyone call for me?"

He paused. "Oh, yeah, this guy Marcus. Asked where you were, so I told him you were DJing down at Buddha Bar."

I stared at my crates, too tired to be angry.

I needed a new roommate, though.

SEVEN

FRANK WALSTON—OR BIG FRANK, as everyone called him—looked like a hero straight out of 1930s DC Comics: tree-trunk arms, barrel chest, and a cinched waist. He ran security for Bill Spector's parties, Sheets and Pillows and True, and his dead-serious affect kept clubland in check. He was born and raised in Alphabet City and had grown up in New York's hardcore punk scene, the lone Black teen shredding skate parks by day, diving into mosh pits at CBGBs by night. He eventually became a bouncer there, too—he'd crack a rare smile reminiscing about the night Debbie Harry turned the club inside out with a surprise appearance. Hardcore kids started half the brawls downtown, but they respected Big Frank, since he came up through the scene with them.

Big Frank had always dreamed of starting his own party—a soul night called Sweet Thang—where he could be the brains instead of just the brawn. To make it happen, he teamed up with a childhood acquaintance from the neighborhood, Marc LaBelle. The grandson of Jews who escaped Nazi Europe, Marc was raised in a mostly Puerto Rican neighborhood on Avenue D. He got his start with Maurice Bernstein at Giant Step, juggling an absurd number of roles: handing out party flyers, overseeing marketing and distribution for their streetwear line, road-managing bands signed to Giant Step Records, even doing MTV and radio promotion for major labels who paid Giant Step to consult and help them gain street cred. With seventeen jobs, it was no wonder he burst into every room like he was fifteen minutes late, even when early.

Marc carried a Lower East Side kid's typical chip on his shoulder. He felt slighted that when rappers shouted out neighborhoods—"Harlem!" "Brooklyn!" "The Boogie Down Bronx!"—the LES got no love. When Marc and Frank reconnected, they decided to put on Sweet Thang at Den of Thieves, on East Houston, to show some neighborhood pride. It didn't hurt that, because Frank's landlord owned the place, they got it for cheap.

Big Frank had heard about me from a friend who'd caught one of my sets. He dug the way I played the original samples from the rap hits, and one day he called me to say that he and Marc wanted to try me out for a few weeks, alongside some other DJs.

"What's your DJ name, for the flyer?" he asked.

A straightforward question that cued my existential nightmare.

Since that first flyer for Surf Club, coming up with a DJ name had become the bane of my existence. House music DJs could get by using their government names. But if you played hip-hop, you had to brandish something mighty and mythical. Mr. Magic, Stretch Armstrong, DJ Hurricane, all the good names seemed to come with a cape and a backstory—like you were out to fight Magneto armed with only a crossfader. My first attempt, DJ Olde English, had sounded clever in my head—like I was pouring one out for the

Bard—but now it had all the appeal of the backwash at the bottom of a bottle gone flat. It had stuck for longer than it should have.

I started explaining to Frank. "Well, it used to be DJ Olde English, but that sucked. Right now, I'm Mark the Spark, which is what my friends are calling me, but I'm think—"

"Kid, I don't need your life story. Just the name."

"Mark the Spark."

This name wasn't even mine to claim. Mark the Spark was an unofficial member of Brand Nubian, whose debut album constantly played at SLAM!, a clothing store on the Upper West Side run by my friend Gideon Harris—six-four, light skinned, with a short Afro, and a perpetual toothpick hanging from his mouth that complemented his laconic stylishness. Gideon opened the shop to inject some downtown flavor into a neighborhood better known for discount outlets like Loehmann's. Like most of us, he came from an eclectic background: His Jewish mother worked as a therapist, while his father, Julius Harris, was a gifted Black theater actor better known for appearing in the blaxploitation classic *Super Fly*. Through Gideon, I grew close with Blu Jemz, one of his best friends at LaGuardia High School, the city's premier public performing-arts magnet school. I'd met Jemz at NASA, but we were both a little too high then to forge any meaningful connection. Gideon became the bridge that brought us together.

By day, SLAM! sold brands like PNB, SSUR, Headhunters, and Triple 5 Soul, as well as my mixtapes—though those mainly collected dust in the front window. At night, it transformed into our clubhouse, a delinquent paradise of weed, malt liquor, and sketchy cocaine that burned like battery acid. Some guys even started

sleeping there, turning SLAM! into an unofficial hostel in violation of many NYC building-code rules. I never stayed the night, but
I spent a lot of time there. It was a spot where Gideon, Jemz, our
friends, and I could do what we wanted. Including listening to a lot
of Brand Nubian—which had earned me the hand-me-down nickname "Mark the Spark."

Put on the spot by Big Frank, it was the best DJ name I had to
offer. I figured I'd never meet the real one, anyway.

I landed the gig, but had no idea how it would play. Hip-hop had
history in the Lower East Side: In the late eighties and early nineties, Kool DJ Red Alert played Tuesday nights at the World, an old
Yiddish theater turned nightclub. The party became famous for legendary performances by Tribe and Public Enemy. Amanda Scheer,
a doorgirl at the World, later launched Car Wash in an abandoned
public high school. But by 1994, the scene had moved on.

Now, the Lower East Side belonged to rockers in motorcycle
jackets, fishnet stockings, and skaters sporting "Zoo York" tees and
baggy Carhartt pants who drank at spots like Max Fish on Ludlow
or Sapphire Lounge on Eldridge. They occasionally drifted into Bill
and Carlos's parties, but they mostly inhabited their own scene.

The neighborhood also had a dark side—the heroin undercur-
rent I'd brushed up against at eighteen, during a brief flirtation with
the drug. I remembered cabbing down to Seventh Street between B
and C to score, sitting on a stoop with a teenage junkie, both anxiously awaiting the dealer's return. Somehow, I knew junk wasn't for
me. But that boy's face—smooth-cheeked and hollow-eyed—still visits me sometimes, and I wonder if he made it out, too.

Den of Thieves had plenty of LES grit, but it also didn't reek of stale beer or look like Richard Hell had been pissing in the same corner since 1974. A concrete bunker, with bartenders who had raven-black hair and more tattoos than bare skin, it would have been the perfect backdrop for a Nine Inch Nails video.

And an unlikely home for a soul party.

The first week, I tag-teamed with a DJ who couldn't hold it down. Whenever I had it going, he'd hop on and kill the vibe. I'd get into a groove and feel him hovering behind me, clutching his next record like an eager schoolkid raising his hand with the wrong answer. He played okay records. He just played them wrong.

What set DJs apart wasn't the records—we all had similar collections. The difference between a dead floor and an electric one was momentum. The art was in the details: when to drop tracks, where to bring them in, how many verses to play. "Shimmy Shimmy Ya" could pack the floor from the first piano note. But "Brooklyn Zoo"? You had to skip that eight-bar intro and bring it in on "I'm the one-man army Ason." With older hip-hop, one verse was enough as people had been hearing those tunes for years.

Among elite DJs, there were two distinct styles: the commanding mic controllers and the masters of clever transitions. DJs like Kid Capri possessed thunderous voices that sounded like they had subwoofers hardwired to their chests. It wasn't just about volume; it was about *presence*. Kid Capri could call out *"IT'S THE KIIIIIIIID CAPRI!"* with no music playing, and people would sprint to the dance floor like it was a fire drill.

White DJs, however, rarely touched the mic. It wasn't that we couldn't grab it—it was that our voices were…wrong. Thin, reedy, nasal—like someone had left the bass out of our entire genetic makeup. If we got on the mic, it was mainly for emergencies. "Uh, excuse me, everyone . . . the white Subaru double-parked outside is about to be towed."

Stretch's genius lay in pioneering a different approach—he crafted routines where he'd drop the volume at key moments, letting the crowd sing the lyrics themselves. This effectively made the audience handle what would usually be the DJ's role on the mic. For white DJs, this was our brilliant cheat code—letting the crowd bring the energy our voices couldn't deliver.

The other DJ I was sharing the set with that night didn't rock the mic *or* kill it with the transitions, and he was gone the following week.

Weeks two, three, and four, I played with a revolving door of great DJs, but my obsessive digging for breaks clicked most with Big Frank and Marc's vision. I loved dropping slow jams like Tyrone Davis's "In the Mood" at peak hour. Those seventies funk ballads—with tough drums, plinkety harps, lush strings, and velveteen vocals—sounded *hard* in the industrial space. "In the Mood" had been sampled by the Beatnuts on "Lick the Pussy," so it was syrupy soul that worked for the hip-hop heads.

At the end of week four, as he handed me my $125 for the night, Frank told me I had the gig. I gave him a pound and hugged him. I needed the job. For my cred, my wallet, and my soul.

"I'll just need to call your mom to let her know."

"Excuse me, *what?*"

"When I hired you," Frank said, matter of fact, "the guy who told me about you said you were fifteen, so I got your mom's number and called her first. I promised her I'd make sure you got home safe." I was mortified. Frank continued, "She asked if I'd put you in a cab at the end of the night and take a picture of the license plate as you drove off."

I stared at him. "You *called* my *mom?*"

"Yeah," Frank said, totally unfazed. "Nice lady. Funny."

I shook my head. "Frank, I'm twenty. I shaved, like, three times this month."

He shrugged. "Good for you."

"Well," I said, heading out, "thank you sincerely for this gig, I love this party. I think we could really blow it up." Halfway out the door, I called back, "Shouldn't you come take a picture of this cab?"

Even if I was the only DJ with a verbal permission slip from his mother, there were worse things than having two good people watching out for you.

* * *

I was doing my best to make it through NYU. Since transferring, I'd switched my major from sociology to music theory and composition. If I could get my academic life to dovetail with my extracurricular life, I thought maybe I'd be able to generate the motivation to stay in school and keep my promise to my mother. One morning, I grabbed a cab to West Fourth Street to squeeze in some practice before my piano performance class. I had no delusions of being a concert pianist, but there was something about the little practice rooms—the discipline, the formality—that I loved. Just a piano and a bench. *Solitude. Control.*

I took out the sheet music for "Comme d'Habitude"—the

French song Paul Anka later turned into "My Way"—and ran it a few times, scribbling the correct letters above the notes to cover for my iffy sight-reading. Half an hour later, my teacher swept into the cramped practice room, pacing behind me in her gray sweater vest and wild bun.

"Yes! Yes! More passion!" she cried, her voice soaring like Seiji Ozawa conducting Mahler's Fifth. I white-knuckled my way toward the song's emotional apex—Sinatra's croon filled my head. I prayed the teacher wouldn't notice the faint pencil marks on the page.

After piano, I walked into history class—a sun-filled room buzzing with thirty unfamiliar faces. Having transferred halfway through sophomore year from Vassar, I'd parachuted into a sea of strangers. I knew a thousand people in this city, but not a soul in this room. That changed after class when I met Stan, a sophomore who invited me to WNYU, where his friend DJ Mayhem ran the top rap show.

Hours later, I stood inside the glass-walled studio, the ON AIR light glowing red. Martin Moore, the co-host, manned the control desk while Mayhem worked the turntables. His long, skinny fingers manipulated two copies of a Roots remix as dexterous as a magician performing sleight-of-hand. His turntablist skills conjured a repeat delay effect, making snares stutter and ricochet like a Pete Rock fill brought to life.

After the show, Stan introduced me to Mayhem, who had kind brown eyes and a trace of a mustache.

"Stan said you DJ, too?" Mayhem asked.

"Just clubs," I said, suddenly self-conscious. "Not that crazy shit you were doing. What was that Roots remix you were cutting up?"

"The Beatminerz remix of 'Proceed'?" he said. "I got it from MCA. I hit up the labels a couple times a week to grab promos. Come with me sometime—I'll get you in the mix."

Maybe NYU wouldn't be a total waste of time after all.

* * *

From then on, Mayhem and I met weekly for our record run, equipped with empty bags ready to be filled. We'd start at the corporate fortresses of MCA, Elektra, and Atlantic—where irritated security guards buzzed us up to bored receptionists who barely glanced up from their magazines. Eventually, someone would emerge, and, if lucky, we'd score a GZA twelve-inch among the unwanted future Frisbees.

Downtown brought a looser vibe. At Tommy Boy's Flatiron office, indie spirit was alive and well. Tom Silverman had founded the label in 1981 with a five-thousand-dollar loan from his parents. With Monica Lynch—a street-smart tastemaker with blazing red hair—they built something unique. Their second release, Afrika Bambaataa's "Planet Rock," fused block party chants with Kraftwerk's electronic pulse, moving six hundred thousand units. Even after hits with Naughty by Nature, Queen Latifah, and De La Soul, they kept their scrappy downtown attitude.

I lingered awkwardly in the doorway of a cluttered room while Fatman Scoop, their head of radio and club promotions—a giant of a man with size 20 Nikes and an even bigger voice—was on the phone, charming a radio programmer into promising to play the new House of Pain single. He spotted us, threw a hand over the receiver, and whispered, "Go to the closet. Make it happen." He spoke to us only in catchphrases, but in his honeyed rasp, they landed like gospel. We darted over to the stash, combing through vinyl like moles burrowing tunnels. I snagged two copies of the *New Jersey Drive* soundtrack album, and whatever overlooked gems were still up for grabs. As we slipped out, Scoop's booming voice followed us—the same one that would one day ignite a million dance floors on "It Takes Two" and "Be Faithful."

Next up was Bad Boy, on Nineteenth Street. It was a new label, but their first two artists, Biggie and Craig Mack, had exploded out the gate. The reception area was packed with DJs, shoulder to shoulder, silent as a dentist's office—all waiting for that precious promo vinyl. The wait never bothered me. Among strangers who shared an obsession, I felt at home.

Finally, we rode down to 160 Varick, where Def Jam operated out of a former printing press loft with thick, creaky floors and towering arched windows. It was a step up from their first office—Rick Rubin's NYU dorm room, where Rubin met Russell Simmons, a savvy rap promoter whose brother was in Run-DMC. Together, they released T La Rock and Jazzy Jay's "It's Yours" and LL Cool J's "I Need a Beat." In 1986, they put out *Licensed to Ill* by the Beastie Boys, the first hip-hop album to ever top the *Billboard* charts. Mayhem and I peered past reception as employees moved through the hallways, excited to be so close to people who were continuing to move culture—this time with Redman, Method Man, Warren G, and Murder Inc.

By the time we left, our bags were bulging and our shoulders aching. Sometimes, Mayhem came back to my apartment, patiently walking me through the tricks he did on the radio, standing over me like a hip-hop sensei. His moves required an incredible amount of coordination. With two copies of the same record, he'd isolate a snare drum on one turntable while the other played the same track. He'd tease in that snare just before it naturally occurred on the record playing, then rapidly release it again—creating a stutter that mimics a triplet digital delay effect—with human feel and precision. Then in one fluid motion, he'd switch hands to the left turntable, scratch it, and drag it back to align both records perfectly, which in itself created a swirling, phasing effect.

My hands fumbled to keep up. Unlike Mayhem, I hadn't spent years practicing in my bedroom. I was spinning at Club USA just two months in. What I gained in reading crowds, I sacrificed in technical mastery.

It was fine, though. Really. Sometimes you need to lean into what God gave you.

* * *

Something shifts in New York clubs when spring arrives. If you can drag a party through the grisly winter months, then in April the party gods throw you, well, a party. Everything changes. The line outside is its own scene—strangers becoming friends, anticipation building with each step forward. And by the end of the night, it's a full-on block party—shiny Lexuses double-parked beside tricked-out Toyota Corollas, a sound clash of Ron G and Kid Capri mixtapes blasting from different cars. People leaning on hoods, drunk, high, trying to score one last phone number before heading home. Sweet Thang, our little soul party, had become the spot. Suddenly, we were cramming 500 people a night into a venue that technically held

250. The space, which, when empty, felt like an urban bunker, was now hot and muggy, the air ripe with sweat, weed smoke, and Issey Miyake perfume.

The club was barely wider than a 747's cabin. The dance floor took up the back half of the space, my booth hugging the right side wall like a diner counter. Each week, the same faces passed, exchanging nods and smiles, though we rarely met outside these walls. Certain songs became our shared language: Teddy Pendergrass's "Believe in Love" and Barrabas's "Woman." I played the downtown standards, too, but this weekly family gave me the freedom to take risks—like the fiery salsa-funk tune "Sonaremos el Tambo," by Latin Tempo. The crowd let me lead them to more eccentric corners of music because they trusted me to bring them back to familiar ground.

Underground hip-hop royalty started rolling up. Da Beatminerz, who crafted all-city anthems for Black Moon and Smif-N-Wessun, were early regulars. Any time I caught Evil Dee's head bobbing during opening sets built on the Nite-Liters, Ripple, and Joe Williams, I knew I was doing good. Guru from Gang Starr would post up at the bar, nursing a bottle of Hennessy, charming every pretty woman within earshot.

I filled my sets with the records sampled by beloved underground rappers. Take Bobbi Humphrey's "Blacks and Blues"—used in the KMD's "Plumskinzz"—Jerry Peters's lyrical piano floating above the ride cymbal, a triangle shimmering in the distance. The song's delicate soul moved me near tears, and I wanted the whole room to feel it.

Or the Ohio Players' "Pride and Vanity." Its hypnotic four-note bass line was used in Mary J. Blige's "What's the 411?" But the song itself soon went somewhere stranger and more eccentric. I'd let it play as long as possible, testing how adventurous the crowd was willing to be.

Then there was "You and Music," by Donald Byrd. That opening drum break hit like a wake-up call, while Byrd's trumpet did the same. And the climbing chord progression filled the room with jazz-funk euphoria.

Al Green's "I'm Glad You're Mine." The Isley Brothers' "Between the Sheets." Mtume's "Juicy Fruit." It was a hip-hop crowd partying to decades-old R&B, but no one cared because the originals hit just as hard. And with the endless gold mine of eighties R&B serving as the source of so many new rap tunes, there was always something new to bust out. DeBarge's "I Like It" for Grand Puba's "I Like It (I Wanna Be Where You Are)." Or their "Stay with Me" for Biggie's "One More Chance (Remix)."

Around 1:30 a.m., I would drop a few new joints—Junior M.A.F.I.A.'s "Player's Anthem," Luniz's "I Got 5 on It," Jodeci's "Freek'n You (Remix)"—and let the room hit a giddy peak before pivoting to something unexpected to close—Stevie Wonder's "Don't You Worry 'Bout a Thing" into Santana's "Oye Como Va." The cha-cha rhythm threw them for a moment until they found themselves singing every word. Mayhem often tagged along to Den of Thieves, especially for the early sets when I leaned into the rare breaks. "You should do this on the show next week," he said. So, the following Wednesday, I hauled sixty of my most prized records up to the station. By 10 p.m., I was setting up on his turntables, my stomach twisted up like a pretzel from nerves.

"What should I introduce you as, Mark the Spark?" Mayhem asked.

"Shit, I dunno, maybe just—"

"Wait, we're back on the air," he interrupted.

Mayhem grabbed the mic. "My friend—Mark—has something a little different for you tonight. Go on, kid."

I dove into a chaotic ballet of vinyl, cueing and dropping tracks in rapid succession. In twelve minutes, I crammed forty or so breaks. At one point, I thrust my hand into a crate hunting for Redd Holt Unlimited's *The Other Side of the Moon*, jamming my fingernail right into the sharp cardboard sleeve. Blood smeared everywhere but adrenaline numbed the pain. Mid-set, the phone lines lit up. Mayhem turned to me: "Yo, Mister Cee just called in. Says you're killing it."

Mister Cee was the legendary DJ who discovered Biggie. *Also a great DJ name.* At the end of the set, DJ Scratch—*maybe the best DJ name*—from EPMD introduced himself and gave me a pound. DJ Scratch, world champion battler, one of the most revered in hip-hop. Even if I didn't have their crazy skills, maybe I had something worthwhile.

* * *

On a Tuesday at Den of Thieves, Gideon from SLAM! tapped me on the shoulder and nodded toward the bar with a grin. "Yo, that's the real Mark the Spark."

I was mortified. At the end of the night, I went straight into the office.

"Frank, I want to change my name."

"What am I? The DMV?"

"No, no, I mean my DJ name. For the flyers. Just make me, uh... I don't know... Spark Ronson."

Spark Ronson sounded like a guy hawking fireworks from the trunk of a Chevy Nova, but it'd have to do.

As I turned to leave, Frank added, "By the way, you played too much hip-hop tonight."

"I only played twenty minutes! You know we've got a hip-hop crowd here. It's a miracle we don't have a riot playing so little."

"I've been dealing with drama and bullshit most my life," he said. "I don't want that here."

I pictured a young Frank, a bouncer at CBGB, his body braced against the stage like a human barricade. On one side, a riotous mosh pit. On the other, Debbie Harry, poised and regal, clutching a mic.

I understood fully.

"All right, man. I got you," I said, pocketing my cash. "See you next week."

EIGHT

THERE ARE PEOPLE WHO ENJOY a night out. And then there are night people—a different kind altogether, the ones who become their best selves once the sun dies down. Sometimes you can tell the difference just by looking at them. You see them in the club, buzzing with an energy that seems to lift them a few inches off the ground. Daytime is all right, but it's just the warm-up.

My favorite night people had an irresistible charge to them. Take Lysa Cooper, who ran Juicy with DJ Belinda. The first time I saw her, I was eighteen, at Soul Kitchen. Lysa looked like she was from another planet of hipness. We became friends, and I discovered her outer magnetism was matched by an inner warmth. Though born in the Bronx, she was as downtown as it got: a muse to Robert Mapplethorpe, a best friend to Keith Haring. (When I met her, she even recalled the night that he snuck me and Sean Lennon into Area.) By day, she styled high-fashion shoots; on weekends, she was the den mother of cool Nolita. Her Crosby Street apartment became a landing pad for newcomers she took under her wing. Sprawled on her worn leather couch, I'd absorb stories of eighties New York—Area,

Danceteria, and The World. "Being a night person," she once told me in her velvety rasp, "it's written in my sign, my chart, and my human design."

Some people blew in and out of the scene on their own unpredictable schedule. Max LeRoy—my childhood friend from the Dakota—appeared and disappeared with little explanation throughout my life. He was so charismatic that whenever I introduced him to people, they'd invariably call me the next day to ask, "So, when are we hanging out with your friend Max again?" He was also sublimely erratic—as likely to give you his favorite jacket as he might give away yours. I once left my Fender Stratocaster at his place and when I came back for it, Max casually explained he'd traded it for some video games. Another time, after we'd stayed up until three smoking opium, Max woke up on my living room floor with his shoulder mysteriously dislocated and promptly began slamming himself into a wall until it popped back in. Then he sat down to watch the NCAA Final Four without comment. I didn't see him again for eight months.

When he was gone, his friends and I would huddle together like an impromptu support group trading Max stories to soothe ourselves. Being around him was so exhilarating—and lifted you so high—that the crash when he left felt almost unbearable. But then he'd show up again like a burst of adrenaline, and for the month he was around, the rest of life went on pause. For Max, nighttime was wilder but kinder—a freedom from the weight of expectations and the life he was supposed to be building instead of burning.

And then there was Blu Jemz. He loved the night, New York

City, and a white-label Armand Van Helden promo twelve-inch with equal devotion. He'd spin for eight people in a dank Alphabet City basement just because the venue had a GSA sound system and was generous with drink tickets. "This party's going to be the shit," he'd say, dragging me into yet another basement. And he was usually right. A hundred of the best parties I've ever played in New York were thanks to Jemz. Even when he wasn't spinning, Jemz held us together. He was the ringleader, pulling everyone to the after-after-party with a glint and a grin. There was no one else I'd rather be standing with on an East Village street corner at 3:30 a.m., breath clouding in winter air, hailing a cab to some after-hours. If you're going to dive so deep into the city's undertow that you'll spend days recovering, you need a wingman like Jemz to guide you.

There was always a duality to this kind of life—a pain lingering under the surface. I'd seen it growing up. Jemz and I had a shorthand: in a rare quiet moment, one of us would murmur, "Tears of a clown, right?" acknowledging the shadow side of our hijinx. You were seeing people at their best and their worst, and there was always a fear that you'd lose balance and tip into the darker aspects of it.

In the first year and a half after leaving Vassar, I'd held it together. Sure, I was teetering, but I made it to class—barely—showed up for family dinners, and passed in the world for a semi-functional human being. Then came the batshit hours of nightclubs like the Roxy and Save the Robots, and my circadian rhythms got thrashed about until I didn't know up from down or night from day.

In 1995, though, you couldn't tell me shit—not while I was doing what I loved and "*doing it well.*" So, being the son of two world-class night people, was gravity pulling me in like a black hole? Maybe. Either way, I bent forward, tucked my knees, reached out my arms, and readied a dive.

Sophocles wrote, "Fate has terrible power." Centuries later, Alicia Bridges more famously declared, "I love the nightlife, I got to boogie...on the disco round, yeah." They both had my number.

* * *

> **Bill & Carlos**
> **Present Saturday Nights.**
> **Featuring**
> **DJ NOT YOU!**

Even with Sweet Thang's success, I couldn't break back into Bill and Carlos's rotation. Each eye-catching new club flyer sitting on the counter at SoHo stores like Union and Stüssy was my harsh reminder.

Their newest party was Honeycomb Hideout, a Saturday night in the grand basement hall of Indochine, the trendy Vietnamese restaurant in NoHo that had served spring rolls to Andy Warhol, Fran Lebowitz, and half the fashion world. I refused to let a bruised ego ruin a good night out, plus my boy DJ Mighty Mi was playing, and if I hung around long enough, he'd eventually need to pee and ask me to jump on. At worst, I'd have my five minutes of glory.

Indochine had two levels. Upstairs was the restaurant, which looked like a lush jungle fantasy with palm-leaf wallpaper, vintage cane-backed chairs, and thick columns that rose from the floor to the double-height ceilings. Waitresses strutted from the kitchen to the bar like they were on a Paris runway. The din of fabulous, unplaceable accents and clinking glasses was so loud, you couldn't tell if the person next to you was discussing Fashion Week or planning a junta. It was decadent and sexy.

Then there was the lower level. Outside, down a stone staircase so precarious that it looked like it should have come with a liability waiver, a man stood with a guest list in front of a bar too cool to even have a sign.

Unlike Indochine, with its gleaming black-and-white checkerboard floors, Undochine kept things stark and concrete. Banquettes hugged one wall; a curvy wooden bar stretched along the other. The low-ceilinged room was dark and intimate in a way that implied they'd either spent a small fortune on a lighting designer or half the bulbs had blown out. I saw the painter Francesco Clemente leaning on the bar, smoking a cigarette. Tom Mello—a famous rave promoter from Boston who had just moved to New York—chatted to Lady Miss Kier from Deee-Lite, her Technicolor aura livening the room. Nearby, graffiti legend Futura scrawled something on a napkin that would now be worth more than my monthly rent. As always, the room housed downtown's secret aristocracy: rap heads, art kids, and just enough weirdos.

I strode in proudly clutching *Rass!*, a rare calypso-soul record by the Jamaican pianist Monty Alexander, eager to show it to Mighty Mi. I'd hunted it down for over a year, ever since hearing Monty's cover of "Love and Happiness" sampled by the Beatnuts. Though I'd never heard the full song, those four bars they'd pinched were musical alchemy—a warm, crackly funk rhythm section, skanking guitar, and Monty on the Fender Rhodes reinterpreting Al Green with chord clusters that could make a jazz theorist weep.

The Beatnuts were as much deep crate-diggers as they were rappers, flipping everything from *canción infantil* (Spanish children's songs) to proto-hip-hopper Rammellzee. Their beats were meticulous sonic collages. For them, rhyming over an unembellished loop was sacrilege. Discovering the right sample was merely the first step: then came finding the perfect kick and snare, the precise syncopation, the careful sprinkling of horn stabs, sci-fi zaps, and kung fu movie dialogue. Like Q-Tip, DJ Premier, and Da Beatminerz, they built their beats as pyramids of sound. Their debut album, *Street Level*, followed this blueprint faithfully; each track was a master class in layering rhythm and texture. Except one.

"Let Off a Couple" broke all their rules, stripping away all that layered craftsmanship for nothing but four naked bars from Monty. No added drums, no subtle 808s, not even a hi-hat. Only the loop itself. The sample was so perfect that they must have thought, *Anything more would ruin this*. They were right. To add would have been sacrilegious, like applying mascara to the *Mona Lisa* just to prove you had been there.

I'd been carrying Monty under my arm all day like a trophy. It wasn't just a record—it was a declaration to the initiated that I, too, was in the know. But as I walked into the bar, basking in my self-bestowed coolness, I froze. There he was—Juju from the Beatnuts. *Actual Juju.*

As I passed by, I angled the record just so, willing it to catch his eye. My peripheral vision strained for any flicker of recognition without breaking stride. In my head, I scripted his imagined reaction:

"Damn, that kid's got the Monty Alexander joint. He must really know what's up." Of course, deep down, I knew better. He probably hadn't noticed me at all.

I had more than a dim awareness of my desperate need to make strangers love me. But there I was, containing multitudes.

I stepped into the next room, and the dim-lit bar opened onto a grand hall with thirty-foot barrel-vaulted ceilings, towering marble columns, and ornate beaux-arts details. Exposed brick and steel sliced through the space, contrasting the Gilded Age splendor. And there, all the way in the back, sat two Technics 1200s and a mixer atop a plastic picnic table, its cheap folding legs hidden by a polyester tablecloth. It was a towering cathedral of grandeur anchored by something you could pick up at Kmart.

Mighty Mi was spinning Raekwon's new stomper, "Criminology." But the cavernous space muddied the battle-cry horns and pounding drums, turning its sharp edges into a boomy haze. A few guys in loose-fitting leathers lined the edge of the empty dance floor, nodding intently. The girls weren't having it, though, hovering near the bar and waiting for something they could dance to. Sensing the disconnect, with a razor-sharp *jhugga jhugga*, Mi swapped in Biggie's "One More Chance (Hip Hop Mix)." The opening Marley Marl sample hit, and within seconds, the floor was resuscitated, and all was forgiven.

Drawn to the booth as if pulled by the magnets in the turntables themselves, I stood behind Mi, hands behind my back, watching him do his thing. If I knew the DJ at a party, I'd spend most of the night in the booth with them. Occasionally, I'd venture onto the dance floor or over to the bar, but neither place ever felt quite right, and I'd soon find my way back to the comforting warmth of the amps and red glow of the Technics' strobe.

I hung out long enough for Mi's bladder to get the best of him. He turned and said, "You wanna get on for a sec?" *Funny you should ask.*

* * *

Shortly after seeing him at Undochine, Tom Mello called me. In Boston, he'd built a rave empire, becoming the biggest promoter on the East Coast. Kids from Vermont to Virginia flocked to his UK-style raves. Now in New York, he'd fallen hard for Sweet Thang and Honeycomb Hideout. He was about to take over the Roxy—a former roller rink turned superclub on West Eighteenth Street—for a Friday party called Together. Rave stars like Frankie Bones and Joe-ski would headline the main floor, and he wanted me and Mighty Mi to DJ in the side rooms.

In Manhattan's sprawling superclubs, house and techno reigned supreme. On the main floor, dance divas held court, while DJs like Mi and me were relegated to secondary spaces labeled simply "the hip-hop room"—a true triumph of imagination.

A few of the biggest dance DJs even had clauses in their contracts banning all other music once their sets began—something I'd experienced firsthand at Twilo, a superclub on West Twenty-Seventh. I'd be pouring my energy into lifting my small dance floor higher and higher when suddenly my sound would cut dead. The crowd would pivot toward me, their faces saying, "What the fuck, dude?"

Then Junior Vasquez's deep voice would boom through every room and toilet stall, teasing the crowd with dramatic suspense for half an hour, pondering if they were worthy of his first song. This, from the man behind the underground anthem "If Madonna Calls (I'm Not Home)." It was pure diva theatrics—and good comedy as long as you hadn't just double-dropped some E and were itching to pull shapes.

The big clubs—Limelight, Tunnel, Twilo—were a reminder that while hip-hop ruled our little corner of the city, the rest of New York City danced to 120 BPM and up. Nowhere was that divide more obvious than at the Roxy.

Walking into the club, you could see the main DJ booth right away: a sprawling fortress of sound, perched on a balcony high above the crowd. Past the entrance to the left of the floor, a stairwell led up to a narrow room called the Skybox—the Roxy's hip-hop room— where the DJ booth was a cramped closet with a glass door that may or may not have once housed mops.

The main booth declared, *"You are the master of this domain!"* The DJ looked down on the pulsing crowd like a benevolent ruler. Three pristine Technics 1200s were suspension-mounted with rubber bands to shield them from the thunder of umpteen subwoofers. Jet-black gooseneck halogen lamps, entirely unnecessary but super slick, stood guard like soldiers. The setup included a pair of Pioneer CDJ-500s—the first CD players to let DJs manipulate digital tracks with the tactile precision of vinyl, thanks to their revolutionary jog wheels. Wall-mounted cubbies behind you housed records. In a booth this palatial, you could burn a few calories just by pacing back and forth all night. Towers of gear with blinking lights made the space glow like a Christmas tree designed by Kraftwerk.

The upstairs booth muttered, *"Good luck, kid."* The dusty, banged-up Technics greeted me like old prizefighters, their tonearms wobbling where the securing plastic had long since broken off. To fix dead channels I had to lick the back of my needles, which tasted like battery acid and stale cigarette ash. Lighting? A single clamp-on task light, casting the subtle ambience of a police interrogation room. The sound system was a lone Crown amp powering two warhorse speakers that had seen better days. There was barely space for me and two crates.

One booth screamed, *"God is a DJ!"* The other offered, *"Also, maybe God is a janitor?"* But, in the end, you found the booth that fit the music you loved—and, eventually, learned to appreciate the rank tang of battery acid.

* * *

For my first Friday at the Roxy, I arrived early to find the managers debating how full the main room should be before opening up the side rooms, as though it were a matter of national security. The rest of us sat around on crates, twiddling our thumbs, waiting for someone to unlock our booths and switch on the amps.

The room was quiet as the night began, so I played eighties R&B classics for me and the bartender. With four minutes of Dennis Edwards's "Don't Look Any Further" as my cushion, I wandered over to the bar to grab a drink.

"Hey, can I get a vodka?" *Actually, better make it two so I don't have to come back for a while.* "Sorry, make it two vodka cranberries, please," I said, pulling out two drink tickets.

The bartender had short, spiky hair and the chiseled looks of someone who could easily play Hot Bartender #2 on the WB. He raised an eyebrow to say, "Two drinks already?" I tried to deflect with a joke.

"It's fine, I've got a high tolerance," I said with a smile.

"Great, because I have a low tolerance for drunk DJs." He was serious.

He shoved the drinks toward me and I made a mental note to send a friend for future rounds.

For the first half hour, people poked their heads in, did a quick lap, and left. At one point, someone came in and left the door ajar, blasting all six of us with the monolithic synth riff of "James Brown Is Dead" by L.A. Style from the main floor. I rushed to shut it, muttering like a maître d' cursing a patron for leaving the door open on a frigid January night.

The start of any set is like treading water. You have to keep people in the room without burning through the big songs. And this is the DJ's dilemma. Playing a massive tune in an empty room is just plain sad. Biggie shouting "Grab your dicks if you love hip-hop" to four people only highlights how dead the place is. A party tune needs a party, or at least a dance circle. Also, the unwritten code of DJing stated, "Thou shalt play a song only once." Repeating big tracks makes it obvious that it's the songs—not you—making the night.

I grabbed my drinks and made a deal with myself: no more than two sips per record. But it was still early, and I was letting full tracks play to kill time. With nothing to do with my hands, my first drink quickly became a cup of ice.

By 1:30 a.m., the room had filled with a lively but random mix. Bill Spector, whom Tom had enlisted to promote the hip-hop room, pulled in his regulars, who mingled with ravers and models—not recognizable ones, but the newbies fresh from Ohio, wide-eyed in their first taste of New York nightlife. After months with my Sweet

Thang family, it was strange to see so many new faces. One thing became clear: This past year of spinning for an in-the-know crowd had sharpened my skills. I could slay this one in my sleep. I whipped through a few quick medley mixes, using clean cuts and wordplay to tear through "Nuthin' but a G Thang," "Gin and Juice," and "Ain't No Fun." Sometimes I'd bust through twenty songs in five minutes, creating a pile-up of records beside me—sleeveless, stacked haphazardly.

At Sweet Thang, these sets kept the crowd hyped. Here, people were losing their minds the way I once did hearing DJ On-E at NASA. Every week from then on, the room was jam-packed. By 2:00 a.m. we hit capacity, so people started showing up earlier and earlier just to guarantee a spot. Also, half of NYC suffers from velvet rope syndrome: the bigger the club, the more people scramble to squeeze into the smallest corner of it. Side rooms, roped-off VIP sections, toilet stalls.

Finally, around 4:00 a.m., the crowd thinned, and soon after, a staff member would flip the lights to tell me, "Thanks for playing. Now fuck off." Riding a conqueror's high with a half liter of vodka running through me, I'd emerge from the booth, triumphant but alone. The room was deserted, so I'd head down to the main floor, desperate to force some fun among the ravers. Nights like this, I was always chasing some action, on the precipice of dangerous behavior, looking to get wasted enough to mute the anxiety and neuroses that had plagued me since I was three.

After a couple of aimless laps of the Roxy, I'd head home defeated, dump my records inside the door, and stumble to the Korean market for cigarettes and a pack of chips. I lay in bed as day broke and a faint gray glow seeped through the black sheets I'd taped over the glass panes, so I grabbed my comforter and relocated to the windowless living room, collapsing onto the couch. The nights that fizzled out like this always felt like a disappointment. In reality, each one was a bullet dodged.

* * *

Tom Mello had crushed it at Roxy for six months—and then the owners got greedy. As his crowds grew, they kept shaving his cut. When he threatened to walk, they tried to call his bluff: "Where are you gonna take three thousand kids?" He knew exactly where, and within a month, he moved his entire operation, me included, to Tunnel—Peter Gatien's eighty-thousand-square-foot freight warehouse turned playground on Twenty-Seventh Street and the West Side Highway. It was a risky move. That first Friday in December, we all held our breath, wondering if he'd made a colossal mistake. Then forty-five hundred kids showed up. I was thrilled for Tom, but not so much for me and Mi. At the Roxy, people funneled into our side rooms like we were the main event. At Tunnel, the side rooms were little more than druggy pit stops.

Everyone knew that it was possible for hip-hop alone to bring in crowds. Sunday nights at Tunnel belonged to Funkmaster Flex and a party called Mecca, run by a nightlife icon named Jessica Rosenblum. Jessica—or "Stressica," as her friends called her—had white blond hair and perfect skin, which she proudly attributed to never smiling.

Back in 1986, when she was twenty, she'd commanded the door at Nell's, a two-story hot spot on West Fourteenth Street. She wore combat boots, stacked bracelets, a short blond bob, and two earrings: a cross in one ear and a heart in the other. Her tongue was sharp enough to terrify half of downtown. A decade later, she was managing Funkmaster Flex, the most powerful hip-hop DJ in the city, and together they had Mecca, New York's landmark hip-hop gathering, with lines stretching for blocks as up to five thousand people tried to squeeze into the Chelsea mega-club each Sunday to hear Flex command the main floor.

Unfortunately, Mi and I weren't Funkmaster Flex. At Tom's party, I was DJing in spaces like the Bathroom Lounge, an echoey subway-tiled room crowded with sinks and bathroom fixtures. It was about as cozy as it sounds. Drag queens would perch to massage calves strained by ten-inch Patricia Field stilettos. Maybe they'd pull out a little baggie, do a bump, and get back up. Around the corners, you'd catch glimpses of people in various stages of ketamine use, from light hallucinations to full-blown K-holes. Another side room I played was less morbid but no less dismal. Bright lights—the kryptonite to good vibes—exposed every face, every crack in the wall, every dusty crevice in the exposed piping.

Tunnel became a grim place for me after work, too. I was overdoing it, mixing drugs like cocktails. One night, I took heroin by accident—sort of (pass me a bag of powder and I never asked too many questions). The club was already dark and disorienting. Now, woozy from the drug, I struggled to make it down the stairs of the main room. I'd take one cautious step, gripping the banister, and wait for the dance floor's green laser strobes to light my next step.

In the VIP, I bumped into the magician David Blaine. Over pounding techno, he shouted, "Wanna see a trick?" I could barely nod but handed him a quarter, which he promptly bit into, leaving a jagged hole through the middle. Then he put the smaller fragment into his mouth. Holding the larger, now-holed coin at arm's length, he suddenly spat—and the two pieces fused back into a single, perfectly intact quarter. Between his mind-bending trick and my mangled brain, the line between real and unreal had blurred.

That blur continued when I stumbled into Save the Robots, a semi-legal after-hours in the East Village that served those who didn't know when to draw the line—or were looking to draw a few more. I spent many late nights there behind the turntables and would love to tell you stories that would haunt you for months, and make you swear off nightlife entirely, but I can't. Not because I won't, but simply because I can't string together more than five memories from that den of insanity. Others I've asked have all said the same.

Robots didn't open till 3:00 a.m., and once inside, we lost all sense of time, mainly because we wanted to. Anyone going *that* hard was out to forget something. The décor was apocalypse chic: the ceiling patched together with plywood and construction paper, holes in the cork walls covered with scraps of mismatched wallpaper, and a Moroccan lantern dangling above the bar. It felt less like a nightclub and more like a hangout for the permanently adrift. The DJ booth was also makeshift—a rickety wooden platform perched above the crowd, accessible only by an equally rickety ladder I had no business climbing up *or* down saddled with sixty-pound crates of records in the altered states I found myself in.

I played very differently there than at my other gigs, warped tunes like "Dancing in Outer Space," by Atmosfear, with its flanged no-wave hi-hats and avant-garde sax solo. Or Bobby Konders's "The Poem"—a meditative house classic whose bass line sank deep into your chest. These songs were full of dubby delays and trippy sounds that mirrored our collective state of mind. At my other gigs, I was caught up in ripping through records and boiling the crowd into a frenzy. Here, I was happy to let the songs wash over a strung-out dance floor that swayed with eyes closed or spun with arms outstretched. I was too wasted to do much more than that anyway.

I never took drugs when I played Sweet Thang. The hip-hop crowd generally kept things cleaner, with weed and alcohol as the only vices. But the nights at Tunnel and Robots drove me to chemical escape. One night, when I was out late and already flying on E, I took a bump of coke. Within minutes, my chest tightened and my left arm went numb. Could I be having a stroke? At twenty? I sat trembling, waiting for the panic to pass, but it wouldn't let up. Tom Mello and his brother, Neil, found me curled up in a corner practically catatonic and drove me home. They tried to joke with me as we drove up Park Avenue, hoping to pull me out of my hole. I gave a faint, unconvincing smile. When we got home, Tom gently tucked me into bed, reminding me of the English nurses who cared for me when I was hospitalized for meningitis as a boy.

These episodes didn't happen every time I got high, but it was becoming a roll of the dice. Since cocaine and paranoia were classic companions, I figured I was just a little more sensitive to it than the others. Then, one time, the night after a panic attack, my friends started laughing about how we'd been ripped off—the blow had been fake.

Clearly, something deeper was getting kicked up. Now when I

did coke, it was only moments before I spiraled out thinking about how the drug affected my childhood—what it did to my parents and their friends, and the dark cloud it put over our house.

The specter of addiction loomed large, already claiming close friends. The three kids who'd joined me in Alphabet City during my brief heroin phase, years back, were still struggling now. Once lively, they now moved at half speed, their faces gray and pallid. I hated how junk drained the color from the people I loved. Alcohol could be just as damaging. I knew older DJs who had to have four or five drinks at every gig—not so much that they were bottoming out, but enough that promoters spoke about them as liabilities—once brilliant, now tolerated.

I was lucky that somehow, I never got completely swallowed up by those currents, as some did. My own neuroses kept me above water. I also had people looking out for me. Big Frank would have thrown me up against the wall and given me a talking-to if he thought I was really endangering myself. Daniel or Alex, too. There were plenty of good people around me. Sure, many were caught up in whatever they were chasing—or trying to outrun—but there was also a sense of community. Nightlife could be breakneck, but there were also moments of grace that, like the music itself, helped me stay connected to something higher, something beyond myself.

I DJed Robots with a resident named Kathleen Cherry, who played house music. She resembled someone from a sixties sci-fi TV show, with blown-out hair and sparkly sleeveless tops, looking like she'd collided with a disco ball going a hundred miles per hour. I can't remember a time when she wasn't smiling, beaming positive energy out to the crowd, like she was the one steady presence there to keep a shield of protection over us all. Her warmth was a stark contrast to the dark, druggy vibe that clung to so many of us.

One brisk morning, we walked out of the club together. I winced as the unwelcome sun appeared over Avenue B. I wasn't ready to be alone and, knowing she lived nearby, I asked if she would hang out with me a bit longer. Her hazel eyes softened. "Sure," she said. We went back to her East Village apartment, where I lay down on her bed until I drifted off. No moves were made, nothing happened. She just took in a lost boy for the night.

Night people could be angels, too.

NINE

CLUBS GAVE US THE BARE ESSENTIALS: turntables and a
mixer. The rest—records, slip mats, headphones, needles—was
on the DJ. Every night, we got to work to find two stripped-bare
Technics 1200s, lying dormant like headless horsemen. Out came
our needles, and with a single twist, we brought them to life.

The clubs never supplied needles because some cost more than
our paychecks, and, given our deep affection for most club owners,
we'd have been pocketing them left and right if given the chance.
Needles were everything—literally the difference between "The
Sounds of Silence" and "Boogie Wonderland." But not all were created equal. What you pulled from your bag said much about you.

I started with the Shure SC35s, the standard issue for baby
DJs, basic but dependable. Then came the M44s. Their chunky
design glued them down to the record, perfect for scratching. The
M44s were fantastic, except for the part where you had to put
them together. *That* was a sadistic test of your commitment to the

art form: wires thin as floss, screws like rice grains that required a screwdriver from an ant's workshop. To top it off, the M44s came in a plastic tube sealed tighter than a drum; ripping it open set off a grenade of tiny parts flying across any room.

The Stantons had a certain appeal, but they skipped too much. I tried the old trick of taping a penny to the headshell for added weight but adorning a pair of Technics with Scotch tape and loose change felt like defacing a Bentley with a duct-taped bumper. Now that I was gigging a shitload, I decided to splurge on some Ortofons: Concorde-shaped marvels that extended like a swan's neck from the tonearm, ditching the headshell entirely. They were sleek, and best of all, they spared the hassle of assembly. Pull them from their crimson faux-velvet box, screw them onto the tonearms, and you were good to go.

Ortofons came in a kaleidoscope of models: the yellow Nightclub, the black-and-red Pro-S, and my favorite—the blue-and-orange Concorde. Steve at Rock and Soul pitched them like luxury cars, rattling off specs with the reverent expertise of a BMW salesman. In truth, no DJ alive could hear the difference. But I loved mine—not for their sound quality, but because they repped Knicks colors. And, let's be honest, because Funkmaster Flex used them, too.

At 10:00 p.m. on a Tuesday in spring 1996, I carried the Ortofons and the rest of my gear through the double doors of New Music Café, a venue on the ground floor of a six-story brick building at the corner of Canal Street and West Broadway, and the new home of Sweet Thang. Our party had enjoyed a great run at Den of Thieves. What started as a crowd of 50 grew to 500 by the end. At New Music Café, the official cap was 650. But we were often cycling 2,500 covers through the door per night. It was nuts—and most likely illegal.

I set my crate down. It was the start of the night, the oxblood lino-leum floor still a blank slate. I put on Bobby Caldwell's "What You Won't Do for Love"—one of my favorite records, and the kind of song that belongs only in the first or last ten minutes of a set. Some songs possess that magic—the ones I play early just for myself, a private moment of beauty before the night's work begins.

I threw on "Reach for It," by George Duke—a virtuosic key-boardist who played with Miles, Chaka, and Michael. The song was a nasty piece of synth funk with Sly and the Family Stone–like gang vocals that I knew from being sampled in "West Up!" by WC and the Maad Circle. At this hour, only the truly dedicated dancers were streaming in, solo or in pairs—a mix of the genuinely gifted and those enviably free of self-consciousness.

Rummaging through my old-school crate, I saw Curtis May-field's grin beaming up from a battered sleeve as if to say, "I got you." His "You're So Good to Me" did the trick. Mayfield's falsetto, Keni Burke's slap-and-popped bass line, and the record's soaring violins drew a dozen more to the floor. The song was nearly seven minutes, but I never played the whole thing. Momentum was everything in those early hours when I couldn't risk losing a single dancer.

Sylvia Striplin's "You Can't Turn Me Away" came next. Its sharp intro drum fill made even the most basic DJ feel like Kid Capri when scratching it in. It was 90 BPM, but its propulsive bass line and stac-cato vocals made it feel faster, which eased the shift into Mtume's "Juicy Fruit" (95 BPM). My whole night was about constantly navi-gating tempos, trying to move through speeds and feels without the crowd ever sensing it's happening. Nobody wants to feel like their feet are on a treadmill.

"Juicy Fruit" clocked in around six minutes, but I played it for four, nudging the pitch slider every thirty seconds to get it up to 99 BPM for the next record, Gwen McCrae's "Funky Sensation." These speed lifts weren't only functional—they gave a subtle energy boost to the crowd, their bodies unconsciously responding as the tempo quickened.

I played seventies and eighties classics until around midnight. As the room hit its stride, I pivoted to R&B. After letting Barry White's "It's Ecstasy When You Lay Down Next to Me" play through a couple of choruses, I blended in Mary J. Blige's "You Bring Me Joy," an uplifting, gospel-infused track with "Ecstasy" as its foundation. Her opening ad-libs hit: *Hey ay ay hey ay ay hey ay ay yay.* The club erupted into a full-on sing-along, and the crowd transformed into a choir. The floor—the Church of Mary—was packed, and the room looked like it'd never be empty again.

Out of the corner of my eye, I saw the crowd ripple as a new group walked in. Biggie Smalls—King of New York—had just showed up. This was a seismic event in our little universe—like a visit from the pope. I caught only a brief glimpse of him—the club's layout was a strange tangle of corners and angles, and from my booth, I could see little beyond the dance floor. But I got to hear about it later, from Big Frank. At the end of the night, we sat at the bar as he counted cash, recounting what had happened.

"So Biggie shows up with forty dudes, like straight-up knuckle-draggers. I'm talking real dudes!" Frank's voice a mix of humor and exasperation. "I had to double-search every one of them, pulling out all kinds of shit! I told them, 'Come on, man, take that back to the car and put it away!'"

Frank laughed, shaking his head. "I told them, 'Look, we're all here for the girls, right?' But they'd just go, 'Nah, we gotta make sure Big is good.' And I'd say, 'Yo, there's forty of you! Big is gonna be just fine.'" His grin widened as he sorted the piles of tens and twenties in front of him.

"Big was smart, though," Frank added, his voice softening. "He knew I wasn't about to let forty dudes march in all at once. So he waited outside, handed me a stack of hundreds, and said, 'It's all good—I'll wait till everyone gets in.' And he really did. He'd stand out there, calm as ever, for a good hour while I trickled them in a few at a time." It was wild—half of Bed-Stuy rolling through while Big just stood there like a king waiting patiently for his court to be seated. Then he'd come in, enjoy himself, and act like none of it was a hassle.

A few months later, the King of New York showed up again—this time, with a prince. Jay-Z had only just released a few singles, but the latest was a monster. The A-side, "Dead President$"—a lyrically dexterous yet melancholic story of the life of a drug dealer—was already an underground classic. The B-side, "Ain't No N***A"—a raunchy but playful battle of the sexes with Foxy Brown—was one of the biggest anthems of the year. The two were celebrating Big's birthday in style, rocking matching white homburg hats that, under the club's lights, gleamed like snow-capped mountains. From my perch in the DJ booth, I watched Jay cut through the room with an assured, magnetic presence, his head low. Later, Frank told us that Big and Jay had rolled up with a hundred guys in tow, creating pure havoc outside.

It sometimes felt like the records in my crates would come to life at New Music Café. Artists I idolized—DJ Premier and Guru of Gang Starr, Grand Puba of Brand Nubian—were regulars. Mike

Tyson, Wesley Snipes, and Leonardo DiCaprio, a young rap fanatic, also came. Most nights, the room was so packed, and I was so locked in, I barely noticed who was there until someone told me at closing time.

Some artists and celebrities were low-key, others couldn't help but make their presence known. One night, Fat Joe brought his protégé, Big Pun. My set went smoothly until around 12:30 a.m., when every fire alarm in the club went off as if Canal Street itself were under siege. I killed the music, scanning the room, trying to figure out what the hell was going on. People froze, security scrambled, and panic hung in the air. After a tense few minutes, with no sign of a fire or emergency, the alarms stopped and the party resumed. But just ten minutes later, the same siren rang out again. Once more, I cut the music, and everyone held their breath as security scoured the club. No fire, no emergency—just another jarring and mysterious interruption.

Eventually, it came out: It was Pun setting off the alarms. The packed club, with its fogged-up windows, sweaty bodies, and stifling air, was making it hard for him to breathe in his four-hundred-pound frame. But Pun was having too good a time to leave. He parked himself near the fire exit, and every time the heat got to him, he'd crack the door open for some relief, tripping the alarm in the process. By the third round, nobody flinched. I kept the music going, and we all partied on like a deafening siren wasn't echoing off every wall.

Some superstars didn't need to step inside to ignite the place. Like the night Tupac was rumored to be outside, trying to get in. The whisper swept through the crowd like wildfire, and for once, even I got caught up in the buzz. Pac never made it inside—could've been a prank, a look-alike, or just door gossip. But I had Quincy Jones's "Body Heat"—the sample behind Pac's "How Do U Want It?"—cued up, just in case.

* * *

Sweet Thang was such a proving ground for club bangers, hip-hop A&Rs came to scout what was hot. One night I met Ian Steaman, an A&R guy from Tommy Boy and a Sweet Thang regular. He told me his story: After graduating Harvard, he wanted to work in hip-hop, but with no industry connections, he sent out a batch of résumés to all the labels for a prized A&R job, expecting little. Tommy Boy's Monica Lynch came upon his letter and was dumbfounded that a Harvard grad would want to work at her indie hip-hop label. She gave him the job.

I told Ian I had an Akai MPC3000—the drum machine and sampler beloved by Dr. Dre and Q-Tip—and a digital tape recorder at home and was trying to get my production career off the ground. He offered me a shot at remixing "Dinninit," the next single from De La Soul.

"Dinninit" appeared on *Stakes Is High*, the De La Soul album that introduced Mos Def to much of the world. The Brooklyn rapper, hailed as the new torchbearer for the sort of politically conscious rap that had helped define A Tribe Called Quest and others before him, delivered a boisterous verse on "Big Brother Beat." The album also showcased Jay Dee (later J Dilla), a Detroit producer whose moody, introspective title track would become a hip-hop benchmark.

"Dinninit" was set to be the fourth single, and now I had the gig to remix it. Back then, hip-hop singles often came with three or four remixes on the twelve-inch. The industry was awash in cash from CD sales and could afford to pay producers anywhere from five to fifty grand for a remix, depending on the name. For DJs, remixes were passports to production, a pathway out of the booth.

Most spun the original, but the remixes found their way to underground college radio and nerdy mix-show DJs who didn't want to play what everyone else was. Occasionally the remix became the definitive version. In the case of the Fugees, this had been a career saver. They released their first single, "Nappy Heads," and it stiffed. But Salaam Remi came up with a remix that blew the doors off. If that hadn't happened, it's entirely possible the band could've been dropped by Columbia Records. And we might never have gotten *The Score*—one of the most inspired rap albums of all time.

A rapper like Fat Joe might seek out DJ Premier to reimagine his song with Premier's trademark sound—those gritty boom-bap drums and precisely clipped samples. Without a signature style of my own, I stuck to what I knew best: digging through records. On Berwick Street in London's Soho, I'd found a promising loop from a rare-groove track by Lowrell.

Ian liked my demo and asked who I wanted to mix it. I had no idea. My production experience didn't extend beyond my bedroom. I knew a mix engineer's job was to take your tracks and vocals and add equalizers and effects that glued it all together, essentially putting your song on steroids. But I didn't know a single mix engineer, so I grabbed the nearest Wu-Tang record and flipped it over and saw "Engineered by Carlos Bess." Wu-Tang's flawless debut album was electrifying, jarringly gritty and abrasive in the best way.

Two days later, I was in Firehouse Studios with Carlos. He

cranked my remix on towering speakers that made everything sound amazing and then spent hours tweaking knobs on a sixty-four channel recording console that dwarfed my eight-track Mackie mixer at home. Then he handed me a digital audio tape of the finished mix and sent me on my way.

Feeling triumphant, I rushed to Tommy Boy with the DAT in hand, ready to blow Ian's mind. But ten seconds into the playback, the room caved in on itself. The mix was murky and dark—everything I loved about Wu-Tang, but completely wrong for my shiny slice of cookout soul.

"This can't be right," I said, my voice shaking. "It sounded great in the studio."

Ian winced. "It's, uh, definitely gritty."

I knew the remix would never see the light of day and I never spun Lowrell again. It stung too much.

* * *

On the far edge of West Twenty-First Street sat El Flamingo, once the Marquee—a black box where, as a teenager, I'd pogoed to Blur's first New York gig and stage-dived with the timid conviction of a kid not quite ready to die. By the mid-nineties, it had been reborn as El Flamingo, a Latin dance club. Despite the rebrand, it was still the same no-frills black box, with splintered wood underfoot and raised platforms for performers. In the fall, those platforms had been shaking under go-go dancers, egged on by feverish crowds. Now, the dancers shivered in their sparkly costumes each time the double doors opened and sent a wintry gust through the place. The dance floor was dotted with a few couples willing themselves into a party spirit.

In winter, we never said it was freezing; we said it was "brick out." And during those "brick" months, I may as well have been called DJ Coat Check. North Face, Triple F.A.T. Goose, Eddie Bauer—every jacket in the five boroughs seemed to find its way to me. Foul-weather friends, acquaintances, and girls I barely knew flashed pretty smiles and asked the same seven words: *Hi, can you stash this for me?* As if the actual coat check was demanding kidneys as payment.

No matter how many times I shoved them down, the unruly pile at my feet refused to stay buried. By midnight, it had grown into an iridescent, down-filled organism—shimmering, shifting, and threatening to consume the booth, the decks, and me along with it. Knee-deep in polyester chaos, I'd be mid-mix, sweating over the pitch control, only for someone to materialize with impeccable timing: "Oh, it's just the black one."

They're *all* black ones.

Mighty Mi and I were playing together, and we were deep into the "let's get drunk and rewrite song lyrics" phase of boredom. Tonight's target: "Dazz," by Brick. Milo shot a John Travolta finger toward the dance floor and deadpanned, "The music makes your body move...they're ALL WHITE!"—a twist on the original's "Well all right"—our acknowledgment that tonight's crowd was whiter than a *Dawson's Creek* reunion.

Two white DJs mocking their own kind like we weren't part of the problem was both dumb and exactly the level of entertainment we needed on dead nights like this. Playing for all-white crowds meant a lot more songs about jumping. Thank you, Kris Kross; thank you, House of Pain.

With no reason for us both to suffer, I waved Milo off and promised to grab his money. No sooner had he left than Sean "Puff Daddy" Combs—the Svengali of East Coast hip-hop and R&B, wrapped in a white fur—strode onto my dance floor. Aviators on. Six disciples flanking him. He paused, scanned the room like a CEO inspecting a failed local branch, and cocked his head at me as if to say, "Puff Daddy's now in your shitty little party. You're welcome."

I turned it on for him and went into overdrive. Total, Biggie, Frankie Beverly, Chaka Khan, Mary—everything I thought he'd dig.

Half an hour in, Puff strolled up to the booth, waving a crisp hundred-dollar bill like I was meant to park his Rolls.

Caught in the mix, I nodded politely. "Thank you. Really, it's enough just playing for you."

"Take the money."

I shook my head. "I mean, with all the hits you've put out, you make my job easy—"

"Man. Take. The. Fucking. Money."

I took the bill.

He leaned against the booth, the louche impresario in full form. His dark shades made him unreadable—a walking poker face. His kinetic energy transformed dead rooms into pure revelry, but something in that power hinted at combustion. He led a conga line of hangers-on out the club's doors. And the night closed down a few weeks later.

When spring came, Sweet Thang got a visit from Biggie, who arrived late one night, rumor had it, straight from central booking—giving new meaning to the term "release party." He was standing twenty feet from me, partying to my music. But even with this proximity, I remained what I'd always been—a superfan. I knew every word of every song. I had a painting of him on my wall and stubs from his concerts in my drawer. I spent countless hours sitting in the lobby of Bad Boy, awaiting his promos. Once, on the way up I shared an elevator with him and Faith Evans, his wife. Too starstruck to speak, I just stood there, grinning. There was something about this three-hundred-pound man from Bed-Stuy—how he made every New Yorker feel proud, even a rich kid from the Upper West Side like me. And then he showed up at my place of work to hear me spin. Often. I doubt he knew my name, but it didn't matter. It was the ultimate validation—from a king.

Even in absentia, he ruled the night. Like the time the head of promo for Bad Boy arrived carrying a gleaming acetate of his latest single. An acetate was the holy grail—a very fragile first pressing, straight out of the lab, the prototype intended to birth every other copy.

"I got the new Biggie joint...Just took it to Flex. I can't let you keep it, but you can play it right now."

I handled the acetate like blown glass. These things were fragile and could easily shatter. Every play wore it down, so I didn't dare rewind more than once while cueing it in my headphones.

As Lil' Kim's "Big Momma Thang" reached its final chorus, I yanked the crossfader over and dropped Biggie's new joint.

A meteor hit the club—the first kick drums landed like sonic booms, punctuated by Biggie's unmistakable wheezy "Uh!" The verse kicked in and the room snapped together, unified by the heft of his voice and a nasty bass line from Herb Alpert's "Rise" beefed up by kicks, snares, and bright percussion. Hearing this song's club debut, we knew it: This was history unfolding in real time. For once, I had no clue what to play next. What could top it?

Several weeks later, I got a call from my friend Josue Sejour, a Haitian Brooklyn rapper who dressed only in velour Fila tracksuits. He came to Sweet Thang every Tuesday with a fellow Haitian named Erick La Peau, who often spun the reggae set. The three of us had a ritual: ending each night with sandwiches on the stoop of my Sullivan Street apartment.

His voice on the other end was thin, brittle, like it could crack.

"Biggie's dead. They shot him in LA."

I looked around my room. He was everywhere—the giant Krylon portrait of him I'd bought from a street artist; my fifties Seeburg jukebox with a 45 of "Big Poppa" with "Warning" on the flipside; a *Vibe* magazine open on the floor, his face staring back at me. I hung up the phone and cried for a man I'd never met.

Biggie's passing left a black hole in hip-hop and the city itself. It also cleared the way for Puffy to become a superstar—an unlikely leap for a promoter turned A&R turned impresario.

Nobody thought of Puffy as a rapper; they thought of him as a force who could will anything into existence, no matter the cost. He took over downtown—and then the Hamptons—until the whole city seemed to revolve around him and his parties. I'm sure he thought I was a great DJ, but on his mission to shake up New York society, it didn't hurt to have a fresh-faced white kid from a nice family in the booth. When I got booked to play his parties, I'd look to the VIP area and see people like Muhammad Ali, Martha Stewart, Denzel, and the Duchess of York all mingling. Everyone went.

It would take twenty years for horrific allegations of what was also going on beneath the surface—abuse, violence, intimidation—to unravel. But what was abundantly clear, back then, was that Puff wielded a tremendous amount of power and cachet. It's difficult to overstate his hold on mid-nineties New York. He made people's careers—playing gigs for him certainly helped mine—and his disapproval meant a certain kind of exile. For all the gigs I played for Puff, he probably spoke five sentences to me. But even to me, the DJ, he emitted a chaotic energy that left me both starstruck and deeply unnerved.

Back then, the only controversy surrounding Puff was around the music. Most DJs I knew were grateful for his records—for those three minutes of pop bliss that made our lives easier. New York had been taking a commercial ass-whooping from the West Coast for years. In 1995, the city produced only two number-one rap albums on the *Billboard* chart. Puffy brought the East Coast back with a run of platinum Bad Boy albums and singles. But he was also a polarizing figure to the underground heads and purists who lived and breathed that grimy New York hip-hop: Smif-N-Wessun, Big L, O.C., KRS-One, Jeru the Damaja. They fucking hated him. For them, Puff's music wasn't hip-hop. The R&B hooks, the obvious samples, the "eh eh" ad-libs he wedged in between every other Biggie line—it was over-polished and coated in seventeen layers of plastic.

Puff got off on taunting them, embracing the title "shiny suit man." The shiniest party of all was his twenty-ninth birthday, at 55 Wall Street. Once the location of Manhattan's Merchants Exchange, the building was a monument to old-world grandeur, power carved into every inch. Cadillac-sized chandeliers hung from sixty-foot coffered ceilings; elaborate classical sculptures sat on dazzling marble floors. Pressing through the enormous brass double doors, I took it all in and had one thought.

Jesus, the sound is going to be atrocious in here.

I set up on the mezzanine balcony, far above the action. A high-strung woman materialized beside me, a walkie-talkie, clipboard, and headset completing the holy trinity of event-planner stress.

"Here's the run of show," she barked. "You play from eight to ten, then Kid Capri takes over, and Puffy makes his grand entrance at ten thirty."

Kid Capri was a legend—a god to every hip-hop DJ who had ever cued up a record. Capri birthed the mixtape game. Before him, mixtapes were dry blends of songs, stitched together with little energy or flair. Capri flipped the formula on its head, cutting up tunes and working the mic as if we were live from the Fun House or the Rooftop—clubs most could only dream of stepping into—even though he was recording in his mom's kitchen in the Bronx River Houses. He didn't just play songs; he set them on fire. And I was going to see it up close for the very first time.

As the first guests arrived, the younger crowd drifted straight to the dance floor—a translucent light box glowing like a bespoke runway, monogrammed with massive *P* and *D* letters, just in case anyone forgot whose party it was. Meanwhile, the older set made a beeline for the roped-off VIP area below me. From my perch on the mezzanine, I could see everything: Donald Trump's windswept combover bobbing above the crowd, Penny Marshall's shaggy blond hair, a couple Knicks players, and Sam Cassell's unmistakably shaped head. I leaned on the classics—Grace Jones, Sister Sledge, Prince—and the floor started filling up nicely, a sea of expensive shoes and designer fabrics catching the shimmer of the light box like a disco snow globe.

Around nine thirty, Kid Capri came in, trailed by a crew of roadies carrying enough records to play Puff well into his forties. He glanced at me only briefly, but I didn't take it personally. He was a Bronx legend. At 10:00 p.m., he gave me the nod. He was ready. I unplugged my headphones, removed my needles, and stepped aside—our ceremonial changing of the guard. Capri faded out my record and launched into his signature intro, cranking the volume up by what felt like twenty decibels and hitting the mic with his trademark energy. *"IT'S THE KIIIIIID CAPRI!"* His voice ricocheted off the sixty-foot ceilings like a cannon blast.

But something was off. The energy shifted, the dance floor started to thin, and I caught glimpses of the VIPs squinting up at the booth, their expressions somewhere between confused and concerned. You could practically hear the murmurs: *What's going on up there?* Perhaps Michael Bolton and the Duchess of York were unfamiliar with authentic hip-hop mic rocking.

Capri was the ultimate pro, but I could feel it happening. I imagine he could feel it, too. He went into overdrive—getting louder, more animated, pulling out tricks that had probably killed from the Bronx to Tokyo. There were a thousand clubs—hell, *every other club*—where Kid Capri would hand me my ass on a Technics direct-drive platter. But this crowd? This weird, high-stakes cocktail of rappers, royalty, real estate moguls, A-list actors, athletes, society types, and supermodels, like a Mase video spilling onto the pages of *Vanity Fair?* This was my bread and butter.

And then, the commotion.

I peered over the booth to see a squadron of anxious PAs, their faces plastered with terror like extras in a disaster movie. Then I spotted Puffy, in a powder-blue three-piece silk suit, clambering up the iron balcony, a man scaling the walls of his own fortress. He looked agitated, shouting something I couldn't make out at first. Then I heard it.

"Yo! Get the other DJ back on! Get Mark back on!!"

A cold bucket of dread poured over me. *Replace Kid Capri? Midset?* This was blasphemy. But Puff's word was law, and there'd be no arguing.

Capri unplugged. I plugged back in. The ceremonial changing of the guard—this time in awkward reverse.

I got back on and the status quo was restored. But there was no celebrating in the booth. Just a dark cloud hanging over us. I pretended to be engrossed in my headphones, adjusting knobs that didn't need adjusting.

I dropped "Mo' Money, Mo' Problems," and as the crowd—smug with having made it to the party of the year—rapped every word of Biggie's verse, I thought back to his first visit to Sweet Thang. No red carpet, no VIP spectacle—just him posted up in the corner with forty of his dudes, vibing to the music like everyone else in the club.

A gig like tonight paid well and would lead to more like it, but standing there amid all this gilded excess and imported marble, watching the industry machine grind on without him, I knew which experience really meant something to me—and it wasn't this one. Postscript: Capri got back on and turned the place out like a legend.

TEN

STOOD OUTSIDE DJ Mighty Mi's apartment building on Lexington and pressed the little white button labeled BERGER.

"Hello?"

"What up, kike? It's me," I said.

Taking after our Black heroes in music, we'd decided to reclaim the slur—a way of turning venom into camaraderie. It hadn't exactly caught on. But we loved it.

"Oh, what up, kike," Mi replied, buzzing me in.

I walked past the mezuzah on his doorjamb—a lone relic from his Jewish upbringing. Like most Jews I knew, he felt close to his heritage but skipped the synagogue part. Besides, hip-hop had been his religion since fourteen, when he'd gone to his first rap show, at the Philadelphia Spectrum. While others watched the rappers, he'd been transfixed by the figure in back—working two Technics and a mixer.

We played a lot of the same parties and bonded over beats, basketball, and *The Larry Sanders Show*, the sharp HBO satire starring Garry Shandling as a late-night TV host. Before long, I was spending hours at his apartment—a lesson in organized confusion. A queen-size mattress was jammed into one corner, crates of records spilled over the floor, and a banquet table buckled under the weight of turntables, a mixer, an Akai MPC, and a sixteen-channel Mackie mixing desk. A studio apartment in every sense of the word.

I perched on the edge of his bed while he crafted underground hip-hop beats between deep bong hits. Mi wasn't just a great DJ—he was the most adept beatmaker in our circle. He already had a Ghostface and Mary J. Blige remix under his belt. Since my dismal episode remixing the De La Soul track, I'd set out to learn more about the mixing process. Watching him work—chopping dusty sixties drum breaks and jazz-fusion bass lines into underground heat—was my production boot camp.

If Milo's apartment was the lab, DJ Jules's loft in the Flatiron District was my history class. Jules had been a mentor since I opened for him at Tilt years earlier. Despite a decade in New York, he'd kept his English accent and an elevated style that made him a sort of hip-hop dandy. Most of us wore Nike Air Maxes or Air Force Ones, blue jeans, and a T-shirt. Jules wore aged 1920s denim, stiff as cardboard, paired with vintage white Converse All-Stars and obscure Japanese brands like A Bathing Ape and Hysteric Glamour that the rest of us had never heard of.

When he first landed in the city in the mid-eighties, Jules began as a barback at MK's—one of the first clubs in the Meatpacking District—founded by Mark Kamins, the DJ who discovered Madonna and produced her debut single, "Everybody." Quickly working his way up to the DJ booth, Jules became a firsthand witness to hip-hop's rise in downtown New York. Spending time with him offered a glimpse into an era when Basquiat was hanging out at MK's and the Beastie Boys were crashing the door at Nell's.

"So, Jean-Michel comes in and hands me this copy of 'Beat Bop'..." he'd say, holding up the first pressing of Rammellzee's single, with Basquiat's artwork on the cover. I'd edge closer, nearly falling off the couch.

My favorite Jules story took place in a Tribeca basement where he was spinning when a massive brawl erupted in front of the booth. As a man got pummeled on the floor, his girlfriend—desperate to stop the music—tore the tonearm clean off Jules's turntable, leaving one of her fake nails lodged in the pitch control slider. And if Milo was the lab and Jules the lecture hall, then Rock and Soul was the newsroom. Once a week, I was in there leaning against the record bins with DJ Chill Will and Ruby Rube debating the Canibus vs. LL Cool J beef like it was our own lives. In some ways, it *was*. Rivalries dictated what records we could and couldn't play. A DJ we knew got yoked up in the booth for playing Tupac's "Hit 'Em Up" at the height of the East Coast vs. West Coast feud—a move so spectacularly stupid, we couldn't make sense of it.

It was absurd to think, given the sheltered way I grew up—at least outside of my childhood home—that I could consider myself any part of these feuds involving real lives, killings, and tragedy, or relate to the emotional weight of it. But there I was, DJing in these clubs two degrees removed from artists embroiled in violence—and with a certain measure of New York pride.

By the summer of 1997, I was a twenty-one-year-old college dropout. My old friends were either still in school or kept hours that didn't overlap with my nocturnal craziness, so I spent most of my waking moments around fellow DJs, finding sanctuary in a tribe who shared an unspoken understanding of the life—the relentless grind, the highs and lows, and the understanding of why spending eight hours elbow deep in dusty crates at a flea market constituted an ideal Sunday.

We came from very different upbringings—kids of rock stars, public servants, immigrants, electricians, and academics—but we all fit a certain mold. First, we were know-it-alls—the good kind, mostly. We could tell you who played drums on Grover Washington Jr.'s *Mister Magic*, where to get the best meal in Chinatown at 4:15 a.m., and how to de-scramble the blocked porn channels on a Time Warner Cable box. The same nerdy obsession that made us walking encyclopedias of DJ Premier samples—like which Ahmad Jamal track he flipped for what obscure Fat Joe B-side—spilled over into many realms of nonessential trivia.

Second, we were all bad with money. If someone hands you two hundred dollars in cash at 3:30 a.m., you're not rushing to Citibank to make a deposit—if you even have a bank account. Every DJ had a secret stash: under the mixer, stuffed in a Nike box, or wedged between crates of records. Few of my friends saved. I was lucky— I had a safety net in my mother. But I also didn't have any sense of where I was going, or what I wanted in life in the grand scheme of things—the kinds of considerations that almost all the peers I'd grown up with were carefully laying out for themselves: college, career, stability, kids. Few DJs thought about tomorrow. Tomorrow was a concept for people who went to bed at 10:00 p.m. For those of us who went to bed at 5:00 a.m., it was always the same day when we woke up—like *Groundhog Day*, but starring Method Man and Debi Mazar, instead of Bill Murray and Andie MacDowell.

And finally, we were always fighting to get paid more while trying to hide the fact that we'd gladly do the job for free. The number of times I told a new promoter: *Don't worry, just hit me with cab fare for now and you can pay me if it gets off the ground.* (It never got off the ground.) We haunted each other's sets like booth vultures, lurking until our comrade had to pee and uttered the four words we'd been waiting to hear, *Hey, wanna get on?* And there we were, DJing for free. Grinning like idiots. We were consumed by our craft and addicted to the adulation. The idea of standing in a club, watching people dance, and not being the catalyst was unthinkable—enough to make our hands itch and our brains short-circuit. So I kept showing up, playing everywhere I could. Sometimes for no money, sometimes on the crappiest setups known to clubland.

Which brings me to the tale of 2i's.

Of all the dysfunctional DJ booths in the city, none was worse conceived than 2i's, a small venue on Fourteenth Street between Seventh and Eighth Avenues, next door to where Nell's once sat. Actually, calling it a "booth" is a stretch. It was two turntables and a mixer bolted directly to a brick wall. What's the problem? Well, people tend to dance *inside* a club. If your setup is nailed to the wall, you're facing the wrong direction.

Staring at walls was nothing new to me. When I was a kid, my mother had a fondness for "corner punishment." Misbehave, and you'd find yourself planted in the nearest one, no matter where you were: home, a friend's house, a restaurant. One time, she left

Charlotte, seven years old, standing obediently in the corner of Mr. Chow on Fifty-Seventh Street while the rest of us piled into a cab. We made it a few blocks before my mother remembered and rushed back to find Charlotte still upright, nose pressed against the shiny lacquer. Given the restaurant's walls were lined with framed Basquiat napkin sketches, it's possible she was mistaken for a child actor in some avant-garde performance piece.

Staring into the brick of 2i's, becoming intimate with each ashy pockmark, I couldn't help but wonder: Was the person who designed this booth out to punish DJs? Or just out to lunch? Because this backwards booth ranked right up there with ceiling-mounted urinals as one of clubland's most baffling design ideas. Booth aside, 2i's had good juju—that indefinable magic that makes one black box boom with life while an identical room down the street sits quieter than a Quaker prayer meeting. In 1997, 2i's played host to several great parties, the crown jewel of which was Purr on Mondays, thrown by Belinda Becker and Bonnie Thornton.

Belinda was a gifted dancer and DJ, a downtown mainstay who'd made her name with Juicy—the "women's strip club"—at Buddha Bar. Bonnie had just arrived from South Florida, at twenty-one years old, hoping to land a spot in Gordon Lish's coveted fiction workshop at NYU. She ended up at Nana instead, a punk-rock boutique on Prince Street, where her job as a buyer plugged her straight into the scene. Before long, Bill Spector was paying her to bring her hip girlfriends to Honeycomb Hideout. That's where she first saw Belinda, gliding across the dance floor, and thought, *I need to make that girl my friend!*

They hit it off instantly, and by the end of the night, they'd decided: Instead of working for men, they'd work for themselves. And Purr was born. The Jamaican dancer and the Southern charmer drew an instant crowd, with Jules and me switching off weekly as their resident DJs. Walking into 2i's was like entering a seventies sci-fi spaceship: The front was a dark tunnel, illuminated by a backlit bar that made hundreds of bottles glow in shades of amber, cognac, and bordello red. Past the bar, there were four walls, some good speakers, and a DJ booth facing the wrong way.

That night, seventy-five people were packed into the back, gyrating to Usher's "You Make Me Wanna...," Jermaine Dupri's sharp kick drum rattling every surface. Suddenly, Danny, the club's manager, came barreling toward me, sweat beading on his forehead.

"The cops are outside! The cops are outside!! Change the music!"

Oh, fuck. The other thing I failed to mention is that, in addition to featuring New York's least- practical DJ booth, 2i's was legally forbidden to allow dancing.

Rudy Giuliani became mayor in 1994 with a tough-on-crime, civic cleanup agenda. He particularly loathed nightlife—his deputy mayor compared clubs to "buckets of blood"—and with backing from conservatives and wealthy residents in gentrifying areas like the Meatpacking District, Lower East Side, and parts of Brooklyn, he set out to dismantle clubland. His weapon: a Prohibition-era cabaret law requiring venues to obtain a license for live music or dancing. Getting one meant navigating byzantine zoning restrictions and costly building requirements that most venues couldn't afford.

Police would harass clubs endlessly. Officers would show up unannounced at 11:00 p.m. at a place like Limelight, demand that security hold the door, and then, an hour and a half later, with thousands of people waiting in line, slap the club with a violation for disorderly premises for having too many people on the sidewalk. Cops could barge into any bar at will. If they found no cabaret license and spotted someone with one hand and one foot in the air at the same time while music is played (yes, that was how 1926 defined dancing), they'd cite the venue, pressuring owners with heavy fines and threats of closure.

Club owners complained about rampant corruption and officers who threatened to throw a padlock on their doors indefinitely unless they opened up the till. By the end of Giuliani's first term, his policies had shuttered fifty to sixty nightspots.

I liked Danny, the club's manager, very much and didn't want this to happen on my watch. So I slammed the fader, killing the music, and scrambled to throw on *Television's Greatest Hits: 70s and 80s* as fast as I could. Most of clubland knew the ruse, but the few who didn't glared at me, like, *What's the deal, dude?* As the opening lines of the *Cheers* theme started to drift softly from the speakers, a few more people looked at me like I was on acid. Four or five cops charged in, their eyes darting suspiciously at the sweaty cluster of people now standing stock-still in the middle of a quiet room. One of them stepped up to me and asked, "Were you just playing dance music?"

"I wish. Tuesdays is 'nostalgia night.' I'm two minutes away from playing bingo numbers over here."

They knew we were full of shit, but with nothing else to do, they turned and headed for the door as Gary Portnoy crooned, "And they're always glad you came…"

Just to be safe, I let *TV's Greatest Hits* roll a few more minutes.

After the theme song from *Welcome Back Kotter* faded, I cranked the volume and scratched in the crisp snare of LL Cool J's "4, 3, 2, 1." For once, I didn't need to turn around to know they were dancing—the floor was shaking.

Purr was popping, but Bonnie and Belinda grew tired of playing cat and mouse with the NYPD. They found a new home—Cheetah, at 12 West Twenty-First in Flatiron—where their people were permitted to put both a hand and a foot in the air. I didn't realize I hadn't made the cut until I saw the new flyer—with only Jules's name on it. It stung. I knew he and Belinda had history, but it felt personal, a reminder that some of my elders in the scene thought my rise had been too fast, that I needed to pay dues.

My bruised ego healed fast, and I went to Purr at its new home, which was bedlam by the fourth week. I rolled up to a heaving throng, four deep at the rope. Puff had just opened his restaurant, Justin's, a few doors down, so the street was jammed with double-parked Bentleys, Vipers, and Lambos. Security barked, "Get back!" and as I got closer, I saw Belinda yelling at a few guys twice her size, her West Indian accent growing thicker as she got more riled up. "There's no way I'm letting yuh in now! In fact, I'm nuh letting ANY more men in 'til a dozen women enter!" She was fearless, even giving Mike Tyson a fierce dressing down for trying to push his way inside.

Belinda often walked the club, and if she found the vibe too masculine, she'd hold the door as long as she liked. Purr's admission policy said it all: $5 for women, $50 for men. Jay-Z once showed up with eight dudes, remarking on the steep entry fee. Bonnie, bold, charming, and a fan, looked up and said, "I'm pretty sure you're going to be richer than I could ever imagine in my entire life." He thought about it for a second, said, "Yup," and forked over $450. Purr was a party by women, for women, and any men inside were reminded of their guest status.

Amid the fracas, I raised my arm to get Belinda's attention and sheepishly pressed through the crowd as she gestured for security to open the rope. "I'm the relief DJ!" I said, apologizing to no one and everyone before pushing through the glass doors.

Inside, the tense door drama melted away. A few hundred people were already spread around the club—a chic black box with mirrored walls, a big dance floor at the center, and plush banquettes along the edges upholstered in, you guessed it, cheetah print. The overhead lights bounced off the banquettes, washing the space in a slow-pulsing purple-gray glow, blurring all faces into something beautifully unified.

I headed straight for the booth to hang with Jules, watching as the early dancers glided across the floor to Gil Scott-Heron's "The Bottle." Among them was Daoud, a graceful b-boy whose dreads whirled with the upbeat Afro-Cuban funk groove—music that belied its grim lyrics of lives destroyed by alcohol. No one in Cheetah seemed concerned with Gil's message, though, least of all Jules, who handed me two blue drink tickets. I made my way to the bar and exchanged them for plastic cups of vodka and syrupy, club-grade cranberry juice.

"Expansions," by Lonnie Liston Smith—a rare-groove classic—pulled me onto the dance floor. I never danced, unless you count standing around, bobbing my head, and reciting rap lyrics as dancing. It's ironic that I got so little joy out of the very thing hundreds of people came to me for week after week. I had the rhythm to play the music, but not the confidence to let go. But at Cheetah, the vibes were impossible to resist, and for once, I forgot myself. Julia, a pretty Dominican girl with long, straight hair and full lips painted a deep plum, was out on the floor with her friends. We danced innocently, though a quiet charge passed between us, like friends with an unspoken crush. She was my age but carried a maturity that made me feel like a boy trying to keep up. I tried to overcompensate, mouthing the words to every song like a rap karaoke champ going for gold, clutching my encyclopedic knowledge of lyrics like a security blanket—hoping to mask my awkwardness.

Back at the booth, Jules ripped off a couple more tickets, and I made another run to the bar. As he sipped through the short red straw, I imagined the liquid coursing through his body like I was wearing X-ray specs. I knew it was only a matter of time before nature called and he'd hand me the reins. Sure enough, he announced his bathroom break, leaving me alone in the booth. I rifled through his crates, skipping over the anthems—which would've been bad manners—and pulled out Manu Dibango's "Soul Makossa" and Jay-Z and Sauce Money's "Face Off," which sampled it. The mix turned just enough heads to give me a low-key sense of triumph before slipping back into the general population.

When Jules returned, he asked if I'd fill in for him in a couple of weeks while he was away.

Hell, yes.

I did a lap around the now-packed club, zigzagging my tipsy frame between bodies like a bumper car—too slow to do real damage but unruly enough to knock into a random big dude, and maybe cause him to spill Henny and Coke down his expensive Iceberg sweater. A liability, for sure.

Up ahead, I spotted Jay-Z, a princely head and shoulders above the crowd. In my head, I envisioned a splendid exchange: I'd compliment his art in some nuanced, insightful way, piquing his interest long enough to casually mention that I was the DJ from New Music Café he'd enjoyed. By the end of the night, we'd be toasting Cristal while he insisted I call him Jigga.

With my inebriated brain still workshopping the perfect intro line, the current of the club heaved me before him too soon, and I sputtered, "I love to play all your songs!" I sounded more like the programmer of a third-string college radio station than the crowd-rocking king of Tuesday nights.

I wasn't even sure if he'd heard: Junior M.A.F.I.A. was blasting, my delivery was slurred, and the flow of bodies kept pushing me forward like abandoned luggage on a conveyor belt. But out of the corner of my eye, I saw him tense up and turn to his six-foot-six friend.

"What'd he just say?"

"Nothing much, probably a fan." The big guy shrugged.

I slunk back into the crowd, letting the current carry me, the alcohol mercifully dulling the sting of humiliation.

* * *

Spy Bar was a sprawling lounge on Greene Street with gold chandeliers hanging from triple-height ceilings, throne-like chairs upholstered in velvet, plush couches, and dark woven rugs scattered about. The décor looked like the living room of a wealthy nineteenth-century opium addict, while the cavernous dimensions hinted at its very different past as a depot for NYC sanitation trucks.

Spy Bar was the brainchild of Kelly Cole, a punk-rock theater kid from rural Indiana who moved to New York City the first chance he got. He had started out working the door at Limelight's Disco 2000—where I had once found myself caught in a teenage K-hole. Since then, the club scene had changed radically. Giuliani and his surrogates had gone after the big clubs and their owners, including Peter Gatien, who, in 1996, was indicted in an extensive federal case that attempted to connect him to the sale of drugs in his clubs. Club USA had shut down; Palladium was sold and demolished to make way for NYU dorms. Limelight and Tunnel survived, but they, too, would get shut down for weeks at a time. Gatien was eventually acquitted—only to be deported to Canada after pleading guilty to state tax-evasion charges.

Another criminal case had also shocked downtown life. Michael Alig, the promoter and Club Kid ringleader, and his roommate got into a dispute with a drug dealer named Angel Melendez and wound up killing him. Alig left his body in the bathtub for days; when the scent of decomposition got too strong, Alig dismembered Melendez and dumped his body in the Hudson River. The murder first surfaced as a blind item in *The Village Voice*, but soon Alig was openly bragging about it. Everyone knew these clubs had their share of debauchery, but the grotesque murder by one of clubland's figureheads had a chilling effect.

At the same time, highly exclusive lounges like Wax, Moomba, and Veruka were redefining nightlife, offering VIPs a place to escape the general population. Moomba, at 133 Seventh Avenue, was the crown jewel: a three-story labyrinth of exclusivity. Just getting past the first velvet rope was a feat. But those who felt smug about getting that far had egos bruised when they discovered that they couldn't make it to the second level, much less the third, where only the most exalted of the glitterati mingled.

Kelly Cole came from the superclub era but saw the writing on the wall. With charm, ambition, and a Rolodex packed with porn stars, Harlem voguers, and rock stars like Alice in Chains and Metallica, he was ready for something big. When someone brought him to see the Greene Street space, most recently a French burlesque club called Kaptain Banana, he envisioned an opulent rock 'n' roll lounge he could run like a three-ring circus.

On opening night, the actress and downtown legend Sylvia Miles surveyed the jam-packed scene and, in her glorious New York accent, told Kelly, "You didn't make it in the theater, so you got involved in the theater of the night!"

To get into Spy, you first had to get past King, the six-foot-six doorman from New Orleans who spoke with a low bayou rumble like Dr. John—if he spoke to you at all. Much of the year, he wore a long white sheepskin coat, but come summer, he might show up in full head-to-toe Yankees pinstripe gear or a three-piece tuxedo. His door policy was just as unpredictable.

Guarding the purple velvet rope, King decided fates with a flick of his thumb over a silver latch. Sometimes he smiled upon us, and our nights were made. Other times, he'd eye me and my friends like street urchins, and with one damning shake of his head, we became invisible to him. But even when we didn't get in, hanging outside was entertainment enough. Watching King turn away Donald Trump and other fat cats was worth the price of non-admission.

The DJs were technically not very good—in fact, some were terrible. Off-key, arrhythmic trainwrecks punctuated by a full minute of silence were the norm. But their taste was impossibly cool: the Dead Boys, the Ramones, and the Buzzcocks. After five years on a steady diet of hip-hop, R&B, and disco, these selections were a breath of fresh air—even if that air came filtered through a haze of Marlboro smoke.

One night, the DJ threw on AC/DC's "Back in Black," a song I hadn't thought about since I was thirteen. Hearing it now, I was floored. The sonic clarity, those guitars slicing through the room like a chain saw. And what was more, it made all these inebriated white people lose their minds, dancing on furniture like they were reenacting the fall of Rome.

Spy didn't have a cabaret license, but that didn't stop anyone. Couches, chairs, tables—nothing was off limits. Eventually, Kelly hired an antiques specialist to work around the clock in the basement fixing the damage, like a battlefield medic patching up velvet casualties.

As I watched this wild scene, a thought crept in: I wonder if I could play this for my crowd. That quickly turned into: I HAVE to play this, this MONDAY AT CHEETAH. The idea was absurd, borderline career suicidal. "Back in Black" at Cheetah? The hottest hip-hop party on the East Coast? No one, *no one*, played anything remotely like it in their sets.

But the seed had been planted. I spent the rest of the week practicing, obsessing, devising the most bulletproof routine to drop it—without ending my career.

We'd soon see.

I rode to Cheetah charged with nervous energy. This was the pinnacle of Monday nights—Janet Jackson, Prince, Missy—they all rolled up. Filling in for Jules was a privilege. I brought even more records than usual, determined not to spend the ride home tortured by thoughts like, *If only I had that Brian McKnight and Mase remix*. I had to *murder* it. There was no chance to redeem myself next week if I flopped.

Cheetah's challenge wasn't just the crowd; it was the setup. The club had a UREI 1620, one of the first DJ mixers ever made. It predated hip-hop entirely, built before Flash workshopped his first scratch. A rotary mixer, it had big round knobs for each channel but no crossfader—a nightmare for hip-hop DJs.

Picture yourself at a stove, each hand on a knob controlling a flame. Now imagine raising one flame while lowering the other but having to keep the overall temperature exactly the same. That's what playing on the UREI feels like. When bringing in a new record, you must fade out the current one in perfect sync to maintain consistent volume and vibe. At the same time, your hands are darting to the pitch slider to keep the tempos locked in—a delicate balancing act that leaves no room for error.

The UREI forced me to focus on tight blends, and that night, I was in a zone. I mixed the Jones Girls' "Nights over Egypt" into Cheryl Lynn's "Encore," and even the Supreme kids—who usually stood sullen on the sidelines, waiting for rap—broke their standoff and hit the floor.

Classics gave way to old school to the new shit: Dru Hill's "In My Bed (So So Def Remix)" into Redman's "Pick It Up (Remix)"—both built off Le Pamplemousse's "Gimmie What You Got"—as the last available inches of dance floor filled up. But as the energy built, so did the weight in my chest.

This was it. The thing I'd been preparing for all week.

Time to put my battle plan into motion.

I launched the assault with "It's All About the Benjamins," by Puff, the Lox, Lil' Kim, and Biggie. The room erupted as Barry White's ominous one-note guitar riff and slowed-down disco hi-hats ignited the crowd. The frontline was secured; morale was high.

As the Lox traded verses, I prepared my next move: "All About the Benjamins (Shot Caller Remix)," a corny hard-rock remix redeemed only by Dave Grohl's thundering drums. I aligned it with the current beat. In my headphones, Lil' Kim rapped over tinny, processed metal guitars, and panic crept in. This maneuver felt reckless, but retreat was not an option.

With a calculated flick of both wrists, I executed the switch to the rock remix at the top of Biggie's verse. Miraculously, the crowd remained locked in, rapping along in unison. Whether they noticed the beat change or not, the line held. I survived to fight the next phase.

My hand hovered over AC/DC. Doubt crept in—*Is this brilliance or madness?* I put the record on the turntable, running it back a few times to ensure precision. The tempos were locked.

Biggie barreled toward the end of his verse:

Squeeze off 'til I'm empty, don't tempt me. Only to hell I'll send thee, all about the Benjis.

And then, I struck. The greatest riff in the history of rock 'n' roll: **DUNT DUNNANNUNT DUNNANNUNT**.

The room detonated.

Never had a more precise sound blasted through these speakers. The three-chord monster intro electrified every corner of the club. For a split second, puzzled looks flashed across a couple hundred faces on the floor. But the groove was so heavy, so undeniable, there was no choice but to go with it. By the time the riff circled back, confusion had melted into delight. One guy's face said it all: *Yo, I can't believe dude is playing this—and I'm actually fucking with it.*

Then Brian Johnson's screaming vocals hit, and the whole club just surrendered. Everyone was in the moment.

It was working.

Using "The Benjamins," the biggest club song of the moment, as a Trojan horse, I'd smuggled AC/DC through the gates of Cheetah. And now, the whole room was getting down to it. Part of me was just relieved no one was throwing shit at the booth, but most of me was exhilarated. We were all breaking some unwritten rule—what a DJ should play, what a crowd should dance to—and we didn't care. We were doing it together. I don't remember how I got out of it or what I played the rest of the night. But nothing was ever the same again.

Until then, I'd been playing a version of everyone who came before me: Manny Ames, Ben Velez, Jules, Stretch Armstrong, Funkmaster Flex, Clark Kent. But for the first time, I'd stumbled across my own thing. I started leaning in, taking chances left and right: Eurythmics, the Smiths, the Romantics, the Stone Roses— even my childhood pinup favorites, Duran Duran.

I'm not saying I was the first hip-hop DJ to play rock 'n' roll. The pioneers—Afrika Bambaataa, Kool Herc, and Grandmaster Flash— made Billy Squier's "The Big Beat," The Monkees' "Mary, Mary," and Aerosmith's "Walk This Way" part of hip-hop's DNA. The Clash's "The Magnificent Seven (Remix)" was a staple on WBLS, NYC's leading Black radio station, in the early eighties. Stretch even played Alice in Chains. But for the last decade downtown, on a real hip-hop night, the closest anyone got to rock 'n' roll was the Stones' disco-era hit "Miss You" or Babe Ruth's breakdancing classic "The Mexican."

I wasn't some devil-horns rock 'n' roll diehard. Sure, I felt a spark of pride when my stepfather's music was sampled by Tone Lōc and M.O.P. But this wasn't about family legacy or borrowed glory. This was about the rush of finding something new and unexpected, and knowing it belonged to me.

From then on, at Spy Bar, Wax, and all the trendy rock 'n' roll spots, I'd jump on the set and cut up Led Zep's "Whole Lotta Love" with M.O.P., Rage Against the Machine with Lil' Kim, Jane's Addiction, Tribe, and people would lose it. They'd never heard any-one play this music *on beat*. The rock 'n' roll DJs would let songs fade out, drop the next one, and call it a night. But when you sustain the beat—never letting anyone stop moving for even a second—and keep hitting them with surprises? You *own* the room. I almost felt bad showing those guys up. They'd given me the idea in the first place. But after a couple of "booth bumps," they were usually the most hyped in the place.

One night, I was spinning DMX's "Ruff Ryders Anthem"—the rowdiest anthem of the moment—and dared to drop "I Love Rock 'n' Roll" for the first time. For a split second, brows furrowed and time froze. But then Joan Jett's double-stroked guitars and those monstrous handclaps hit, and the place erupted. Suddenly, Lil' Kim was on top of a leather banquette with her hands in the air, and Method Man was right alongside her, swinging his sweatshirt over his head like a victory parade. Let's be real—I wasn't exactly playing Captain Beefheart. Every rock record I played was iconic, but there was a science to dropping them right. And getting it wrong was an open invitation for a bottle to come flying at the booth.

Months later at Cheetah, filling in for Jules, I ran the AC/DC mix again, feeling smug as the crowd went wild.

Then I felt a hand on my shoulder.

I turned to find a Hispanic dude in an oversized leather coat leaning over the Plexiglas partition from the banquette behind the booth.

He looked pissed. I clocked the scene at his table: a silver bucket with an open bottle of Moët, two pretty girls, both glaring at me like I'd insulted their dead grandmother.

With a slow cadence and just the hint of a grin, he said, "What the fuck are you playing, white boy?"

Okay, it wasn't for everyone.

ELEVEN

I N THE FALL OF '97, Tommy Hilfiger stood before us like a prophet readying his disciples for a glorious mission.

You are the chosen few and you shall go forth across America and spread the gospel of my colorful sailing-inspired apparel. And you shall travel into the great malls of Philadelphia, Atlanta, and Dallas appearing in the garments which bear my name. And Mark, you shall spin music to put the crowd in great humor. By morning, you shall grace local breakfast shows and speak of my work. And by night, well ... if you choose to support the artistry of the local exotic dance community, better I know nothing of it. Nonetheless, I look forward to seeing you a fortnight from now in the promised land of Beverly Hills. Godspeed.

He stepped off the bus, the doors closed, and thus began the Tommy Jeans Tour.

Well, not quite like that. I don't remember if Tommy showed up to wave us off. But that was the vibe: six buzzy it-kids from New York and LA crammed onto a bus to conquer the malls of the American heartland.

I first heard the name "Hilfiger" in Grand Puba's "360° (What Goes Around)" in 1992. Rappers like Puba prided themselves on rocking and name-dropping brands before the mainstream caught on. Back then, Tommy Hilfiger was chasing the yuppies and WASP market with a more colorful spin on Ralph Lauren. Ralph owned hip-hop fashion. Walk into a club like Red Zone, and half the crowd—and the line outside—would be decked out in "Lo."

Still, the hunt was always on for the next big thing. Tommy's bold colors and loose-fit khakis caught on with hip-hop's early adopters. Puba wore it. Q-Tip wore it and rapped about it on Mobb Deep's "Drink Away the Pain (Situations)." So did Raekwon on "Criminology." But the breakout moment came when Snoop Dogg wore a Tommy Hilfiger rugby shirt during his debut *Saturday Night Live* performance.

That night, Tommy Hilfiger came home from dinner, turned on the TV, and called his brother Andy.

"Hey, turn on NBC. Snoop Doggy Dogg is on *Saturday Night Live* wearing my shirt!"

"Yeah, I know. I gave it to him."

What Andy left out was that he'd had to break into a storeroom the night before to grab the shirt per Snoop's last-minute request. The next day, that same rugby sold out across the country. Hip-hop had made Tommy white hot.

It wasn't in their original gameplan, but Tommy and Andy embraced it. They brought in Peter Paul Scott—a hip-hop club dancer, DKNY model, and rapper in Ten Thieves—to shape their marketing. That's how I got in the mix.

I met Peter Paul at Sweet Thang in 1995 under inauspicious

circumstances. He marched up to the DJ booth and, with no short-age of hubris, requested his own song. I liked the track but didn't have it with me. He gave me a look of intense disdain and stormed off. But we got friendly soon after.

Around this time, Ten Thieves had fizzled out, and Peter Paul, who had a young family, needed work. He sweet-talked his way past the front desk and into the Tommy showroom, hanging out every day, folding clothes and dressing mannequins. After a few weeks, Tommy Hilfiger finally approached him.

"Excuse me, do you work here?"

"No, but I should."

His hustle paid off. Tommy liked his style—and his nerve. Peter became Tommy's connection to New York culture, advising Tommy and Andy on who was wearing their gear, which trends were bub-bling, and which rappers and pop stars they should be dressing. Peter floated the idea of casting his friend—a young, white DJ with downtown cred—in their next campaign. I'd done some modeling before—mid-level gigs where I knew the photographer. A Tower Records ad, a *Dirt* magazine shoot with Chloe Sevigny shot by the video director Spike Jonze. The closest I ever got to the glamorous life was an Isaac Mizrahi campaign shoot with Dewey Nicks, a witty high-end fashion photographer, alongside my old friend Ethan and a fourteen-year-old Natalie Portman—newly famous after her star turn in *The Professional*.

Ethan was the real deal—with an angular face and soulful gaze that seemed to reveal his deepest truths, even from a glossy page. Dewey liked having me around as his music-talking comic relief while the pros perfected their smolders.

Mizrahi wasn't as charmed. He'd wander over periodically, gently repositioning me farther and farther out of the shot until I was practically in the next zip code, my back to the camera. Eventually, a production assistant politely suggested I call it a day and sent me home.

Tommy and Andy Hilfiger went for Peter Paul's idea. Next thing I knew, I was photographed in a campaign that featured one of fashion's most batshit lineups: me, Jodeci, Ivanka Trump, Simon Rex, and several others. The following year, Hilfiger cast me once again, this time to play DJ in the brand's upcoming campaign, starring Kate Hudson, Jesse Wood, Kentaro Seagal, and Kidada Jones— a nineties nepo-baby dream team. The shoot took place on a rooftop in industrial Los Angeles. The crew buzzed around, tweaking klieg lights and makeup stations, while the catering team arranged a thousand cubes of rubbery cheddar.

I spotted my equipment—a stack of red metallic cases stamped with s.i.r. rentals in white lettering—and dove in. Kneeling down and settling into a familiar ritual, I unpacked preamps and power amps from their foam cocoons and tore open velcro zip ties. Setting up gear satisfied both the audio geek and control freak in me. I'm sure that, deep down, in situations like these, it also soothed my ego to imagine myself signaling to the rest of the crew that I was a very serious professional with very serious work to do. If I looked like a silly spoiled DJ-model-man out there, it was *only part of the act.* I understood the gaffer's plight.

I lugged two stands to opposite corners of the roof and hoisted the six-foot speakers into place with theatrical grunting to broadcast my effort. Then came the dance of the wiring: XLR cables from the speakers to the Crown amp, quarter-inch cables from the amp to the preamp, and into the Rane DJ mixer. Finally, RCA cables linking the turntables to the mixer. One task remained—the final, crucial step of every DJ setup: grounding the turntables.

I've never met a DJ who understands the science of grounding, but we all know the stakes. Every turntable comes with a thin black wire ending in a horseshoe clip—the grounding cable—which must be attached to a small metal screw on the mixer. If it isn't, you summon "The Hum," a relentless low-frequency buzz that vibrates your soul out of your body. It's not a sound—it's the angry ghost of faulty wiring, here to ruin your dance floor.

As with most rented gear, the horseshoe clip was missing, leaving a frazzled tangle of copper strands. It took me ten tries to get it fastened. Once I did, I pushed up the fader and the sound of Roy Ayers's vibraphone from "Searching" floated into the morning air.

There's magic to playing outdoors. Music becomes something else entirely when it escapes into open air. I liked the idea that my selections might catch a stranger's ear and subtly alter the course of their day—a sentiment both altruistic and embarassingly self-important that captures the contradiction at the heart of being a DJ.

I said hi to Kidada Jones, the main stylist at *Vibe*—the magazine started by her dad, Quincy Jones—who was also a model and consultant for Tommy. She was a gravitational force of style and charisma, effortlessly cool in a way that made me feel like I was at the wrong lunch table in a John Hughes film. She had dated Tupac and vacationed with the entire Wu-Tang Clan in Hawaii for an episode of *Vibe TV* in which she filmed Ol' Dirty Bastard serenading dinner guests at the Four Seasons with a surprisingly tuneful rendition of "Blue Moon."

She then introduced me to Aaliyah—a completely surreal moment, even for me. At just eighteen, Aaliyah had already recorded the most otherworldly R&B of the decade. Her music with Timbaland and Missy Elliott—her genius producer-writer duo—sounded like it had been beamed in from the future and redefined the genre. "One in a Million" was my favorite. When I first brought it home, I put the needle down and my room dissolved around me. Delight, confusion, melancholy, and awe hit all at once. The kick drum wobbled my speaker stands, the 808s shook the ceramic floor tiles. And then there was her voice: dreamy, haunting, intimate, and gorgeous.

Kidada introduced us, Aaliyah smiled, and I kept it together. Then, Kidada, who was less than impressed with Aaliyah's wardrobe options, launched into no-nonsense stylist mode. She grabbed a pair of men's underwear and some giant fabric scissors, and snipped away until, voilà, a stylish bandeau emerged. Then she cinched a pair of two-tone men's jeans around Aaliyah with the smallest belt she could find.

Hours later, the photographer, Sante D'Orazio, fired away as I spun Aaliyah's "Back & Forth," while Kidada and Kate Hudson danced for the camera. Sante pulled me from the decks for a few frames, positioning me between Kidada and Aaliyah. I awkwardly draped my arms around the two. The song faded out and I bolted back to the booth, relieved to be once again behind a fortress of gear.

During the lunch break, Aaliyah wandered over to the turntables, curious, and asked to give them a try. I cued up Too Short's "Buy You Some" and handed her the headphones. She moved her hand back and forth over the record, and when her scratching blurted out of the speakers, she let out a giggle warmer than the LA sun.

I seized the unexpected one-on-one moment to ask her about Timbaland and Missy—how they made music that sounded like it was coded in a language that hadn't been invented yet. She shrugged and said, "They're just…cool," as if talking about an aunt and uncle who let you stay up late watching TV, not the architects of an entire new sonic universe. "I'll introduce you sometime," she added. I knew it was unlikely, but I told her if she did, I'd give her unlimited DJ lessons in return, earning another sunlit giggle.

Later that night, I hit a club called Dragonfly to see a DJ named AM. People were calling him "the West Coast Mark Ronson"—a comparison that irked and intrigued me. At the door, a wiry guy with a mustache was screaming about how he "eats fools" directly into another guy's face. In New York, I could gauge how bad things were about to get. But violence in LA had its own dialect. I couldn't decide if I was about to witness a fistfight or the opening shootout from *Menace II Society*.

I got there late, but AM's set was solid. He mixed Stevie Wonder's "I Wish" out of Nice & Smooth, which reminded me of something I'd do. He smiled and bopped his big frame around the booth. I went up and shook his hand. The guy had skills, and I couldn't pretend otherwise. Still, the vibes in LA were weird. On my way back from the booth, someone who looked a lot like Mark Wahlberg stared me down for no apparent reason. At 1:40 a.m., the bartender announced last call. Someone explained that clubs in LA close at 2:00 a.m., which convinced me that this city and I were fundamentally incompatible. Night people here had to work for it.

* * *

Back on the East Coast, Sweet Thang, which had been running for three years, moved locations again, to Rebar, on Sixteenth and Eighth, owned by the Dorrian family, Irish American bar royalty. (Their uptown spot, Dorrian's Red Hand, had gained infamy as the place where, in 1986, Robert Chambers, the so-called Central Park Strangler—aka the Preppy Killer—was last seen with eighteen-year-old Jennifer Levin, whom he murdered later that night.) By the time I got to high school, Dorrian's was still a magnet for preppy under-age drinkers, though the clientele never appealed to me. Rebar was more my style: a weathered-wood bar flowing into a backroom dance floor.

Sweet Thang's success had a downside. A hip-hop party can only stay under the radar for so long before the "knuckleheads," as Big Frank liked to call them, show up. Dudes dressed in camo who like to start fights. Our original mission statement—"classic soul with a touch of hip-hop"—was now a distant memory. The ratios had reversed. Our crowd at Den of Thieves and New Music Café had always vibed to the early part of the night: Barry White, Loose Ends, Curtis Mayfield. Here, they just stared up at me with impatient faces that said, "When are we getting to the hip-hop?" When a party blows up and starts bringing in larger crowds, people inevitably want the big tracks. To keep the dance floor moving, a DJ's selections skew toward a new median—trading musical discovery for mass appeal. You can't stop the shift—you can only hold it off for so long.

Rebar's long and narrow design caused a precarious bottleneck. It was too crowded, and the testosterone in the room was off the charts. From my elevated booth, I'd look down at the mass of bodies below and see someone weaving their way through the crowd, clutching two drinks, and I'd think, Please, God, don't let anyone bump this guy or a bloody brawl will go off.

When it did go off, April, our bartender—who looked like a homecoming queen who could take you in arm-wrestling—would jump onto the bar with a fire extinguisher and start hammering any of the combatants over the head. Security had to protect the fighters from April more than each other. I'd reach for Marvin Gaye's "Let's Get It On" from my ready stack of post-brawl cuts (I always had a few after-the-fight records ready near the front of the crate). Yet for all the chaos, there was something electric about playing to a club that rowdy and packed—"easy killings," we called it.

One night, around 1:00 a.m., I dropped a new cut called "Déjà Vu (Uptown Baby)." Only a few weeks old, its hometown pride refrain had already taken over every club and radio station in NYC. When the chorus hit, as the crowd chanted, *Uptown baby, uptown baby, we gets down baby...* loud enough to be heard five blocks away, I ducked the volume and dropped the instrumental of Busta Rhymes's "Put Your Hands Where My Eyes Could See" on beat under their voices, remixing the room itself. There was a half-second delay as their brains processed what just happened, and then—they fucking ignited like an energy rocket from floor to ceiling. For eight bars, it felt like we'd all leapt into another dimension.

A friend later told me that, in that moment, Stretch turned to him, shook his head, and said it sounded "crazy." It was my first compliment from the pioneer of this style of crowd control and it meant everything.

At the end of the night, I went to get paid. Frank was counting cash with the weight of the night written all over him. "You played too much hip-hop tonight," he said for the ten thousandth time. It used to be funny. Now it was just the truth.

"Frank, I don't know what to tell you. This *is* a hip-hop party now. We had a good run, but it's not what it used to be."

I don't know if he heard me.

"By the way, I'm not gonna be here for a couple weeks. I'm going on this Tommy Hilfiger bus tour to DJ in malls and shit."

I grabbed my cash, gave him a pound, and walked out the door. With the bittersweet understanding that my time at Sweet Thang— the party that had given me my name—had come to an end.

* * *

TOMMY HILFIGER BUS TOUR 1997

"The Mall Crawl Tour"

TALENT:

Ethan Browne	Rashida Jones	Mark Ronson
Kate Hudson	Kentaro Seagal	Simon Rex
Kidada Jones	Jesse Wood	

TOUR MANAGER:

Rashida Jones

CREW:

Andy Hilfiger
Two New York publicists
One security guard

TOUR LOG

Monday, September 15
Macy's Herald Square
New York, NY

Notes:

- Fashion show opened with Kidada, Kate, and Aaliyah strutting down the runway to "Not Tonight (Ladies Night Remix)" by Lil' Kim in baby-blue windbreakers.
- CNN reporter, reaching for the hard-hitting journalism his producers surely expected, asked eighteen-year-old Kate Hudson if splitting the atom ranked among her goals in life after the tour. "Sure," she replied, unfazed.
- Rashida, fresh off her Harvard graduation, took charge as tour manager, keeping the "bus on the road"—as Andy said— for a hundred dollars a day. Fortunately, the driver who actually kept the bus on the road was earning union wages.

Tuesday, September 16
King of Prussia Mall
King of Prussia, PA

Notes:

- Barely onto the NJ Turnpike, the bus was already engulfed in weed smoke. Security called Tommy HQ, alarmed. Andy, a seasoned bass player who'd seen worse touring with seventies rock legends Blue Öyster Cult, shrugged. "Welcome to life on the road."
- The crowd at King of Prussia Mall—one of America's biggest malls—was confused, expecting actual celebrities.
- The bus was declared a biohazard and sent for fumigation.

Wednesday, September 17
Lenox Square Mall
Atlanta, GA

Notes:

- Aaliyah rejoined the crew, dazzling the crowd with a performance.
- Jermaine Dupri hosted an after-party, followed by a trip to the world-famous Gold Club strip joint. Mark sat across from Charles Oakley, power forward for the New York Knicks, in the champagne room, holding court like Caesar in all-white with a dancer on each thigh. He also caught Dennis Rodman, power forward for the NBA Champion Chicago Bulls, and Michael Stipe, lead singer of R.E.M., sprinting around the balcony to Madonna's "Deeper and Deeper."
- A reporter from *Peachtree This Morning* boarded the bus the next morning. She interviewed the talent, determined to know if they had inherited any of their parents' abilities. Kentaro, an Aikido black belt, offered some Zen wisdom. Mark got nervous and panic-sang "Hot Blooded" before clarifying, "I'm here to spin, not sing." Simon cut in, "And I'm spinning too...from all the love on this bus!"

Friday, September 19
The Esplanade Mall
New Orleans, LA

Notes:

- Andy—a man starved for musical companionship—gave out free guitar lessons on a Tommy Jeans-branded Gibson SG guitar. His lofty goal by the end of the tour, everyone should be able to play at least the first four bars of "(Don't Fear) The Reaper," by Blue Öyster Cult.
- Someone tried to shame Simon Rex for being the only one who got here on talent alone.

Sunday, September 21
Cracker Barrel
Somewhere Off I-20, TX

Notes:

- A local couple in matching overalls and straw hats sharing a tall stack of pancakes barely batted an eye as talent piled off the royal-blue tour bus with AMERICAN TOUR across the front and pictures of the group dressed in neon streetwear down the sides.

- "Where are we?! I don't know! The middle of bumfuck Texas somewhere," one publicist yelled into her phone, silencing the restaurant. Several members felt embarrassed to be from New York.

Tuesday, September 23
Fiesta Mall
Mesa, AZ

Notes:

- The fridge on the bus was now bare except for a lone jar of Hot Balls spicy gobstoppers.

- After appearing on *Good Morning Arizona*, a famished Kidada, Rashida, and Jesse piled out of the bus and into the TV studio to devour a breakfast of sesame chicken prepared by the guest chef at seven in the morning.

Wednesday, September 24
Caesars Palace Forum Shops
Las Vegas, NV

Notes:

- What happ...[redacted]...

Friday, September 26
The Grove
Los Angeles, CA

Notes:

- Tour bus pulled up to the Sunset Marquis in West Hollywood. Legitimate rock legend Johnny Ramone was completely confused as to why he had to give up his table at the Whiskey Bar for a bunch of fluorescent nepo babies.

* * *

Back in the city, private bookings flooded in: a Durex condoms clothing launch with Antonio Sabato Jr., a Fort Greene loft party for Mecca and Enyce streetwear founder Tony Shellman, a gathering at a preppy gay furniture designer's Upper East Side apartment. There were so many gigs, some nights I walked into venues with no idea what the event was even for. It didn't matter—I could tear down any room.

At yet another random fashion gig in a photo studio by the West Side Highway, a six-foot-six bald Black gentleman in wire-rimmed glasses and a perfectly tailored suit came up and asked my name. I realized it was RuPaul. He said, "You DJ so good you're making my booty hurt." It was the ultimate compliment, the drag queen equivalent of a Michelin star.

People often wandered up and asked for my business card. *Business card?* I looked in the yellow pages and found a place on Lispenard Street that made them. They didn't have any DJ logos to emboss, but I spotted one for a stretch limousine that caught my eye. I had them put "Mark Ronson: The Stretch Caddy of DJs" with my phone number. At the top, I added my star review: "'You DJ so good you're making my booty hurt'—RuPaul." All of my "business" decisions were made on the fly, dialing Delancey Car Service on the way out of one place just to make it to the next, always racing the clock. I was twenty-two years old, working eight gigs a week, without a manager, and barely holding it together.

One night, spinning at Veruka, a swanky Broome Street lounge frequented by Denis Leary and half the Yankees, the owner, Noel Ashman, asked if I could play Thursday. I told him I was booked. My sister Samantha, who was standing nearby, volunteered herself. "Have you ever DJed before?" he asked her.

"No," she replied, "but I've stood next to him enough."

That was qualification enough for Noel. Samantha had great taste and a keen musical ear. I knew she'd be fine. She was twenty, with a rebel streak I envied. She had tattoos and didn't suffer fools—the middle finger was her favorite form of communication, just like our dad. She once told Puffy to fuck off when he tried taking her table at Spy Bar, while I frantically tried to wave her off from the booth. She attracted kindred spirits, like Bijou Phillips, who is enshrined in Spy Bar lore for snatching a cigar cutter from some hedge funder and cutting off part of his finger.

Charlotte was our steady center, the only one on track to graduate from NYU now that Samantha had dropped out, too. She'd show up where Samantha and I DJed but knew to head home at two, not five. While we chased nights, she built a fashion business. It started with tank tops she customized while still in school—splitting seams, adding eyelets, threading suede laces up the sides. Friends loved them, then designers and stylists caught on. When Serena Williams wore one of her pieces on the cover of *Sports Illustrated*, orders for C. Ronson exploded. Her apartment with Samantha transformed into a makeshift studio, packed with fabric scraps, scissors, and FedEx boxes as she raced to meet demand.

We were each carving our own path, but beneath it all was something unshakable. A fierce bond born from countless mornings entertaining each other in our bedrooms while our parents recovered from the night before. We knew each other in that bone-deep way that only comes from sharing the distinctly atypical way we grew up. Witnesses—and disciples—of the same universe.

I got booked to play a Broadway charity event at Manhattan Center's Grand Ballroom. Some of my DJ friends would've rolled their eyes at the gig, but I loved the challenge: walking into a room loaded with suits sipping wine and figuring out how to crack them open. What record would it take, how long before they were dancing like lunatics, drenched in a sweat they never imagined when they left the house?

That night, it was *The Jeffersons* theme song, "Movin' on Up," that turned the room upside down. Broadway legend Nell Carter was leading the charge, arms stretched toward the ornate ceiling, shouting the lyrics like a revival preacher.

Then I spotted someone: a small figure in shades, flanked by two massive men, weaving her way along the balcony toward me. As she got closer, I saw it was Aaliyah.

"What are you doing here?" I blurted out.

"I'm going upstairs to the studio to meet Missy and Tim. Come with!"

A few flights up from the ballroom were the Manhattan Center recording studios. The balcony was a shortcut for her to avoid the throng.

My stomach clenched. I looked down at the crowd, now a sea of joyful, sweaty professionals who'd probably canceled tomorrow's breakfast meetings. There was no way I could leave this packed floor and my station unmanned. But there was also no way I could pass up a chance to be in a room with legends from another musical galaxy. I looked back at her, already halfway to the exit.

Aaliyah turned one last time, her expression clearly asking, "Are you coming?" I grabbed the longest record I had—the extended version of "Love to Love You Baby," by Donna Summer, a sixteen-minute disco-sex odyssey. Was it enough time to cover my absence? Who knew? I threw it on, ripped off my headphones, and ran to catch up. Guilt and anxiety churned inside me as I left the booth, but I kept telling myself it was worth it.

I followed Aaliyah into the studio—a warm, wood-paneled room, with a mixing console at its center. Leather couches lined the back wall. Missy Elliott sat on one. An unmistakably Timbaland instrumental blasted through the speakers. Aaliyah slid in next to Missy, who began singing in her ear, pitching a melody to her. Across the room, Timbaland was deep in conversation on a StarTAC cell phone.

He noticed me staring and gave a nod. Missy smiled warmly, and Aaliyah got up to hug me one last time before I slipped out. I ran back down to the booth, just in time to cue up the next track.

TWELVE

I FELL IN WITH ANOTHER GANG of night people: stand-up comedians. They were a lot like DJs—nocturnal, world-weary overthinkers, consumed by their craft and hooked on the fleeting approval of strangers. A comedy junkie raised on *Spinal Tap*, *Monty Python*, and *SNL*, I spent hours at the Comedy Cellar, nursing a two-drink minimum while my new friends Jordan Rubin, Godfrey, and Ardie Fuqua worked the room.

I was introduced to the scene by Jordan, a talented young comedian who—with his wavy reddish-brown Caesar haircut—looked like a Beastie Boy overdue for a trim. I watched Jordan's act so much that I practically had it memorized. The Cellar became a ritual for me. I stopped by after early gigs, lugging my records down the narrow stairs past headshots of Adam Sandler, Chris Rock, and Jon Stewart. One night, I burst into the room mid–Dave Attell set, carrying my metal crate like a forklift. The room was packed, pin-drop quiet, and every eye shot toward me. I froze in the doorway. Behind me, a guy with a buzz cut and bulging biceps slammed to a halt.

"Oh, look," Dave said in his dour drawl, pointing us out, "it's the bomb squad, and they brought their robot."

The room erupted in laughter. I, "Robot," found a seat.

DJs and comedians have a lot in common. Our job is to bring joy to a roomful of people who've paid for a good time, no matter how we're feeling—whether we've just been dumped or our dog got flattened by a Toyota Camry. We both work nightclubs. What DJs call rhythm, comics call timing, and, in both trades, the difference between killing and bombing comes down to a hair's breadth of precision. When we kill, we get a roar—a sound so addictive, we're always chasing it, painstakingly crafting our sets to hear it again and again. For me, the formula is simple: Wait for a line in the song everybody knows, duck the volume, let the crowd sing the line, drop an even bigger record right on beat.

Comics and DJs can also lose the crowd in a heartbeat, our desperation suddenly exposed for everyone to see. Then we go home, haunted by the face of every disappointed audience member until we fall asleep.

We also both finish work in the wee hours, flush with a wad of cash destined to vanish by morning. That was exactly the scenario when Dave Chappelle bounded up the steps of the Cellar one spring night in 1998 and announced that he was headed to a club called Life, a new hot spot on Bleecker.

At this point, Dave had been in *The Nutty Professor* and on *Arsenio*. He was close with Jordan, and I'd seen him perform often. Dave came to Rebar on Tuesdays to hear me play. If Dave said he was going to Life, it sounded like a good time, and I knew him just enough to tag along.

Simon Rex—a fellow comedy fan whose off-key charm had landed him a gig as an MTV VJ—jumped in: "Oh, I know the door guy there. He's my boy. I can totally get us in." We headed south. As we approached the rope, Simon pointed to a towering Black security guard and said, "That's my guy I told you about. Hold on..."

"Yo yo, what's up, man. It's me!" Simon called out confidently.

The bouncer barely glanced at him. "Nah, man. I don't know you."

"Yo..." Simon leaned in, lowering his voice as if to shield Bleecker Street from this privileged exchange. "Remember last night? You didn't let me in but said to come back tomorrow, and you'd take care of me?"

"NAH, MAN! BACK UP!" The bouncer's roar sent Simon reeling. A few moments later, as I was already mentally halfway to a turkey burger with cheese at Waverly Diner, the bouncer clocked Chappelle and went from scary enforcer to eager fanboy. "Oh, what up, Dave! I didn't see you there!" he said, smiling. "How many you with?"

Dave motioned to the three of us, and we got stamped and guided downstairs to a skinny VIP room that was likely an old maintenance corridor redecorated to resemble—well, a much swankier maintenance corridor. Plush dark carpet, deco sconces, and a few banquettes lined each side.

The walls were beige, and so was the crowd: professionally hot people with year-round tans, some with sweaters draped over their shoulders and glinting silver cable bracelets. These were the same types that I had found in past years at model lounges like Buddha Bar and Flowers. But the culture had evolved. Now, there was bottle service.

Bottle service culture originated in the 1980s in Japan, where wealthy patrons could reserve tables at high-end lounges and nightclubs by preordering bottles of liquor. The practice spread to the South of France, taking root in places where the rich vacationed.

By the 1990s, bottle service made its way to New York City. High-end lounges like Moomba, Spy Bar, and Life realized they could make a killing by charging patrons hundreds or even thousands of dollars for wildly marked-up bottles of champagne and vodka. Dance floors, once the focal point of a club, became less important than seating arrangements, and the culture shifted toward a static, hierarchical environment where social status and ostentation dictated the mood of the night.

This wasn't the downtown I first discovered—it felt more like Saint-Tropez via Greenwich Village.

In the background, a DJ named Sophie spun electro-lounge duo Kruder & Dorfmeister, though at this low volume, they might as well have piped in Hitler's Reichstag speech. No one would've looked up from their bucket of Belvedere.

I spotted Steve Lewis, the clubland legend who once ran all of Peter Gatien's superclubs simultaneously. The last time I'd seen him, I was a scrappy teenager playing side rooms at Club USA, Tunnel, and Limelight. He might have remembered me that way, too—he hadn't hired me since. But I couldn't help being drawn to this unfiltered nightlife legend.

Steve had the brusque countenance you'd expect from someone who managed a thousand employees and oversaw as many as twenty-five thousand patrons through the door every week during his Gatien days. But beneath the bark, he was a loving general—blunt in battle but fiercely loyal to any soldier who worked hard for him.

In the old days, I'd swing by his office during the week to pick up my modest paycheck and end up hanging out for hours, watching him shout orders into the phone while winking at me to signal he wasn't *that* mad. Being around him was like tuning in to Steve TV—edgy, amusing, and oddly educational. Only a childhood in Queens and a life lived downtown could have forged this no-bullshit, artful rogue capable of running an empire of adult fun houses that served the masses while staying cool enough for the weirdos. He now ran this place, so I thought I'd try my luck.

"You should let me play here," I said. (Sure, I just spent a paragraph trashing the clientele and décor, but if there was so much as a boom box in the toilet, I wanted in.)

"We already have Sophie. She's great."

Sophie was tucked into a corner behind a black DJ coffin. She definitely knew her shit—playing weird, obscure exotica. Her look also matched the vibe. With fine porcelain features, hair swept into a chignon, and a dark lace dress that screamed "Victorian Steampunk," she looked avant-garde and alluring, which was what half these lounges cared about.

She daintily placed another chic, downtempo track into the tray of a Denon CD player while the sub-frequencies of pounding house music coming from the main dance floor rattled the walls—reminding us of an adjacent room that no one here ever hoped to set foot in. To the rich and famous, the entire club Life existed within this exclusive hallway. If you couldn't get in here, you might as well head back to wherever you came from.

"You see a lounge, but I see a room with speakers and people who could be dancing." I grinned.

Steve shrugged me off. But I was persistent—and I'd noticed that Sophie had a small baby bump. So I kept bugging him. Every week.

One Friday around 9:30 p.m., I was at home when the phone rang.

"Sophie's water broke. Do you want to play the VIP tonight?"

I was out the door by 9:45 p.m., and in purely professional terms, I tore the motherfucker down that night. As I pulled out routines and tricks, turning the carpeted corridor into a dance floor and macassar ebony banquettes into leather trampolines, it struck me that most of them had never heard a decent hip-hop DJ before. It was too easy.

There was no going back to ambient lounge music after that. Steve hired me for the next week and the week after that. Once word got out that the VIP room at Life was a hip-hop party, it was on. Each week, I'd look up from the turntables to see Chris Rock, Mariah Carey, Jay-Z, Rick Rubin, and Prince parade past me on the way to their tables. These people were gods to us, but some of the club's uptight promoters had a hard time adjusting to the new clientele and tried to get me fired every week.

But Steve had my back, and in a few months, these same promoters saw it: This was the most exciting energy in New York and where the scene was heading. They quickly got with the program.

Steve shook things up by bringing in the SKE crew—Justin Salguero, Shawn Regruto, and Richie Akiva—as promoters to draw a younger crowd. They'd grown up together in Independence Plaza, Tribeca's subsidized high-rises. Their teen years mixed skateboarding, rapping, tagging, and running several borderline illicit downtown hustles.

Since then, Justin (Juske) had become a fashion photographer, mentored by the late Davide Sorrenti. He had just shot Eminem for

Rap Pages. Shawn studied film at SVA, his genuine talent and vision pointing toward the thoughtful auteur he would become. Richie, whose dad was a major South Bronx retailer affectionately dubbed "Jew Man" by Fat Joe, was a thoughtful, savvy kid with plans to take over nightlife while dating supermodels.

For fun, they printed up a hundred T-shirts emblazoned with MODELS SUCK in big block letters—a tongue-in-cheek nod to their "fuck the world"–meets–"come on, Barbie, let's go party" ethos. The tees were an ironic jab at the same fashion culture they wanted to infiltrate. People flipped, and they ended up selling thousands and printing bumper stickers.

Once Steve hired them to promote at Life, something ignited. Shallow as it sounds (and it was), this melting pot of unkempt youth, slick fashionistas, blingy music icons, and the occasional Hollywood royalty made for a wild and noisy decadence every Friday.

No one soundtracked the new New York nights like Jay-Z. After Biggie's passing, there was no question who the best rapper alive was. While Puff had the commercial dominance, Jay had artistry, and his authentic credentials enthralled the white kids fascinated with street culture. His output was relentless—and pure fire: "Ain't No N***a" with Foxy Brown, "Can't Knock the Hustle," "Who You Wit," "Can I Get A…," "Brooklyn's Finest" with Biggie, "Money, Cash, Hoes" with DMX. But only one record made New York's prettiest partygoers sing out like off-key theater kids in a middle school musical.

When "Hard Knock Life (Ghetto Anthem)," with its woozy, rugged beat and genius *Annie* sample, dropped in Life's jam-packed VIP, the endorphins of so many people belting in unison unleashed a collective euphoria. With Jay-Z himself holding court at table 1, cooler than the ice in his champagne bucket, there was no question who now ran this town.

The track's producer, Mark the 45 King, had crafted classics like "The 900 Number" and Queen Latifah's "Ladies First" before falling on hard times. He was living in a halfway house when he saw the film version of *Annie* on TV and had the idea to flip it. He took Charles Strouse and Martin Charnin's lily-white show tune, "It's the Hard Knock Life," and injected it with swagger and soul. Now, Jay had done the same with this lily-white club. The floor was so packed that waitresses could barely maneuver through it to deliver the endless parade of bottles from the bar. This room was surely a fire hazard, but no one was leaving. They'd spent their whole adult lives trying to get in here.

As the last chorus hit—*'Stead of kisses, we get kicked...*—I ducked the volume, letting the crowd scream, *It's the hard knock...* Then I dropped DMX's "Ruff Ryders' Anthem" right where the word "life" would have been. They roared.

* * *

Summer of '98 was a movie. Wesley Snipes was Hollywood's biggest action star and an OG hip-hop head who spent many a Tuesday night posted up at the New Music Café's pool table. At a career peak, he convinced New Line Cinema to bring his five favorite DJs on tour with him to promote *Blade*—where he played a leather-clad hero who runs around nightclubs slaying ecstasy-chomping, oversexed vampires.

Our crew was stacked: Kool DJ Red Alert, the legendary Harlem-born hip-hop pioneer; DJ Jules, the Kangol-rocking UK soul boy; me, the mild-mannered long-limbed upstart; Doug E.

Fresh, the beatboxing party igniter; and DJ Kaori, the Japanese femme fatale who rocked the mic in broken English and scratched with airbrushed three-inch acrylics.

We cheered each other on at the packed Supper Club in NYC and faced half-filled rooms at the Castle in Chicago, where our NYC party-rocking style—quick mixes and East Coast classics like Mobb Deep and Raekwon—fell flat with the polo-and-dress-shoes crowd. Chicago had its own cool scene, but they weren't showing up for a Marvel movie after-party.

After the *Blade* tour, Hilfiger flew me to LA to spin the opening of their new flagship store. Ol' Dirty Bastard was there riding high off his summer smash "Ghetto Supastar (This Is What You Are)." Stranded after sound check, I got instructed to ride back to the hotel with Dirty and his crew.

I squeezed into the back of their rented SUV. After a few blocks, Ol' Dirty, riding shotgun, passed me a black StarTAC flip phone and said, "Get me Jimmy Levine on the phone."

Ah, he must think I'm some random record company intern. Given that most record company interns are gawky white kids dressed vaguely hip-hop, I forgave the mistake. But...who was Jimmy Levine? *Ah! Jimmy Iovine!* I mentally applauded my detective work.

I had no idea how to reach the chairman of Interscope Records, so I dialed 411 and was connected to the main number. I asked for the office of Jimmy Iovine, which felt like calling Disney World and asking for Mickey. To my surprise, a secretary answered: "Hello, Jimmy Iovine's office."

"Hi, I have Dirty for Jimmy," I said—the silliest string of words I'd ever uttered.

"Sorry?"

"Ol' Dirty Bastard for Jimmy Iovine, please," I repeated. Still pretty silly.

"I'll get him for you."

I handed the phone back to Ol' Dirty, brimming with accomplishment.

Heading east on Melrose, it was clear we weren't returning to the hotel anytime soon. This was concerning, seeing as I had no cab money and had to DJ in three hours. On the other hand, being kidnapped by the Wu-Tang Clan was easily the coolest thing that had ever happened to me.

We parked and hit every sneaker store on Melrose. Dirty and his crew modeled the latest Air Force Ones and Jordans, occasionally asking my opinion. *Yes, 60 Second Assassin, I think the chutney yellow really brings out your eyes.*

We made it back to the Sunset Marquis just in time for me to grab my crates, throw on a fresh shirt, and head out again—like none of this insanity had ever happened.

* * *

Back east, after five years grinding with Sweet Thang, the Roxy, and Cheetah, I'd finally proved my mettle to Bill Spector. Carlos, his old partner, had left the club game entirely, but Bill had assembled a new crew of promoters, and I'd worked my way into being his go-to DJ—the position Stretch had held in the early nineties. Paying those dues the old-fashioned way had meant something. And the reward was equally sweet.

Unlike most night people, Bill was as good company at 2:00 p.m.

as he was at 2:00 a.m. Away from the door drama and velvet ropes, he'd transform into a walking encyclopedia of nightlife lore. A SoHo afternoon with Bill felt like trailing the unofficial mayor of downtown: He'd stop to greet every third passerby, each hello carrying its own story. We'd rendezvous at the Thompson Street playground with our Alidoro paper-wrapped sandwiches and settle onto the stone benches. There, between bites, he'd tell me about Mars, the World, the Latin Quarter, and the night a giant melee finally shut Sheets and Pillows down.

I was spinning his new Wednesday party at the System one night when Q-Tip entered the booth and began wordlessly rummaging through my records. Only a few people on earth could get away with waltzing into my booth and treating my collection like a Sunday yard sale. Q-Tip was one of them.

He'd made some of my favorite music since I was fifteen, his voice and beats part of my life. Over the years, I'd seen him around at record fairs and clubs, but we'd never had a conversation. The club was rocking, and I barely had time to turn around, but my heart spiked.

He pulled out Weldon Irvine's "We Gettin' Down" (the sample from Tribe's "Award Tour") and raised an approving eyebrow. I must've passed his Electric Kool-Aid Record Test, because he took my number and suggested we do something.

Days later, his iconic pinched timbre came through my answering machine. I played it five times in a row, hit save, and called my fellow superfans Max and Daniel and told them to come over immediately.

Daniel arrived first. "Is it a new beat?" he asked, with the muted enthusiasm of a best friend who'd been forcefed one too many of my demos. "Better," I said, walking to my Sony cordless. I pushed play.

[BEEP] *Yo, Mark. What up, it's Tip… It was good meeting you, let's talk about that spot. Call me on 917-XXX-XXXX.* [BEEP]

"HE SOUNDS JUST LIKE ON THE RECORDS?!"

I replayed it. Twice.

"Did you call him back?" Daniel asked.

"Hell, no. What do I say? I'd have to script it first. I can't have Q-Tip thinking I'm some herb."

"Dude, call him."

* * *

Tip and I grew close that summer, cruising around in his Range Rover while he expanded my musical horizons, introducing me to Angela Bofill's prog-soul "Angel of the Night" and Paul McCartney's synth oddity "Temporary Secretary." He played me Radiohead's "Just" and I was spellbound by the entwined guitar harmonies of the bridge, rewinding the same ten-second passage over and over as he careened through Holland Tunnel traffic.

We started a weekly party at Punch—a small Moroccan lounge in Flatiron with white plaster walls and a two-hundred-person capacity. By 11:00 p.m., there were three hundred people packed inside and another few hundred out front. We had underestimated the draw of Q-Tip. Here was a guy who could fill Madison Square Garden, rocking a room of a few hundred. Though new to DJing, Tip's rhythm and selections were flawless, and when he touched the mic, people lost their minds. Myself included. What musical lottery had I won to be here?

At the peak of the night, a fight broke out and people sprinted for the edges of the room, accidentally forming a gladiator ring for two dudes already trying to kill each other. I cut off the music and some very big guys from the Nation of Islam, Tip's security, surged in from all sides. The fight was broken up and the dudes removed, and I quickly threw on a post-brawl classic, Bob Marley's "Three Little Birds."

Another night, I joined Tip at Spy, where he was spinning for a Prince party. The Purple One held court on a plush throne, his security filtering a stream of women into the VIP. Spy Bar had finally upgraded its gear, with turntables and monitors that I cranked to ear-splitting levels—the only way to catch a vibe when you're twenty feet above the throng.

DJs push monitors to dangerous volumes for legitimate reasons: partly to feel connected to the crowd below, partly because music genuinely does sound better loud—our ears perceive more bass and treble at higher volumes. But standing next to the sonic equivalent of twenty chain saws had consequences. Nights like that left a ringing C6 in my ears that kept me up for hours and lingered much of the next day. If I had back-to-back gigs, the ringing compounded. We all suffered. DJ AM ran his monitors even louder than me, his tinnitus so bad he slept with a hair dryer on his bedside table to drown out the constant ring.

I pulled *Off the Wall* from its sleeve, ready to drop Michael Jackson, when Tip stopped me with a raised arm. "Uh-uh. Can't play Michael here," he warned, nodding toward Prince. Musos and nerds loved to talk up the Michael–Prince beef. A friend had a VHS of a 1983 James Brown concert at the Beverly Theater in LA where

Michael jumped onstage for an impromptu verse of "It's a Man's, Man's, Man's World" and an electrifying dance number. Then, Michael whispered something to James Brown, and the Godfather called Prince from the audience to join them. Prince, clearly intent on stealing the show, went buckwild—ripping a shirtless guitar solo, dancing his ass off, and finally swinging from a ten-foot stage prop before appearing to fall offstage. He was clearly out to win the night.

For these two geniuses going head-to-head in the eighties, I imagined the rivalry ran deep. Now I knew it to be true, learning it firsthand, twenty feet up in a former sanitation depot turned swanky opium den. (Years later, I learned another Prince DJ lesson when I played his song "Sexy MF" at a party he threw. His security rushed over to scold me—Prince, now a Jehovah's Witness, had banned profanity in his presence. I asked if "Jack U Off" was still kosher.)

I put Michael back in the crate and mixed in War's "Galaxy," but the intro's fluctuating tempo got away from me, and the beats clashed just enough to earn me a withering look from Prince. Nothing like rhythmic judgment from a musical deity.

After, we piled into Tip's Rover with his friends Beyoncé, then the lead singer from Destiny's Child, and Mos Def. They all cracked each other up speaking in Gullah. For obvious reasons, I kept my mouth shut and looked out the window.

Tip dropped me outside 74 Franklin Street in Tribeca, where I now lived with my friends Rashida Jones (who had managed the *Tommy* tour) and Galt Niederhoffer. Rashida was a talented actor who had just graduated Harvard with a degree in religion. While she was at school, we talked music for hours, bonding over a shared love of Steely Dan. She blew my mind when she told me that their song

"Peg" was rumored to be about her mother, seventies heartthrob Peggy Lipton. Galt was a director whose film *Myth America* (starring Rashida) was making waves on the indie film circuit. I hadn't known them long, but they were two brilliant women who seemed like they'd be running Hollywood in five years—and crucially, they had enough to cover rent. Our airy duplex had pink satin couches and a twenty-foot bamboo that owned the living room. My room was on the top floor, with its own entrance. The arrangement spared them my late-night crew traffic but also cursed me to climb a hundred or so stairs.

I made it to the top and set my crate down, drained. These nights of spinning the same tracks for the same hundred faces in lounges where nobody danced left me hollow, like a jukebox automaton trudging back to its storage shelf until the next performance. The gigs were getting glossier, the crowds sparklier. But sometimes, I missed the days of playing clubs with an actual dance floor.

* * *

Amy Sacco opened Lot 61 at 550 West Twenty-First Street in West Chelsea, on a block better known for sex workers and leather bars in a neighborhood dominated by warehouses, many now defunct. She found a former brewing company with cheap rent. If the club failed, she figured she'd convert it into a vast open-floor-plan apartment. Having recently lost her fiancé, she needed the distraction.

The cavernous space was striking and utilitarian: steel beams, exposed brick, raw concrete. Amy envisioned a modern take on a 1920s Paris salon, a gathering spot for artists and creatives. But instead of Cole Porter at the piano and Picassos on the wall, she had me spinning Jay-Z records, the bass making her enormous Damien Hirst paintings tremble. And rather than occasional visits from *les gendarmes*, she dealt with Giuliani's notorious dance police, who'd storm in to harass staff, rifle through the register, and search pockets for baggies of blow.

Lot 61 had no dance floor, reflecting New York's drift toward celeb-centric lounges—it was essentially a giant art gallery turned cocktail lounge serving small plates, the DJ equivalent of dinner theater. It shouldn't have worked. But it did. The place carried a self-congratulatory vibe ("How amazing are we all to be in here?"), but still managed to go off nightly, largely thanks to Amy, the six-foot-one Jersey girl turned den mother of Chelsea. Wearing a casual glamour that never overtook her realness, she darted between tables looking after everyone, holding back hair while girls who'd had one too many drinks hunched over toilets, watching over her flock with a Garden State groundedness that cut through any pretentions.

I played Mondays with the SKE crew promoting, and Q-Tip would often join me on the decks. One night, he dropped the Intruders' "I'll Always Love My Mama"—a Sound of Philadelphia disco gem with a heavy bass drum and rousing horns.

A big dude came jogging up the stairs, breathless: "Puff wants to know what this record is."

"I. Don't. Know," Tip replied so dismissively that Puff's minion didn't think to look down at the twelve-inch spinning right below his nose. He slunk back downstairs, dreading Puff's reaction.

Tip turned to me. "I just sampled this for a joint with Raphael. No way I'm letting Puff put his shakers and triangles all over it."

(The resulting track, "Get Involved," was well worth protecting the sample.)

When I first started going out, in 1992, places like Tunnel, Club USA, Webster Hall, and Limelight were still the beating heart of the city's nightlife, and you saw all of New York. Their huge dance floors mixed rappers, plumbers, pop stars, suits, designers, artists, and registered nurses. It was a continuation of the downtown energy of the eighties—punk meeting rap, fashion colliding with breakdancing, everyone genuinely curious about each other's worlds.

By the late nineties, when the exclusivity of Moomba, Lot 61, and Life's VIP room reigned supreme, this spirit was disappearing. Different scenes still mingled, but instead of wanting to understand each other's art and fashion, people were more interested in figuring out how the other was getting money—and how to tap in.

The SKE crew were good kids, true downtowners, obsessed with hip-hop and trying to get paid. They were building on Bill Spector's blueprint: skaters, hustlers, designers, models, rappers mingling in the club. But in this money-centric evolution of where music and nightlife were headed, a lot of the normal people and the eccentrics and artists got squeezed out. No Supreme employee or Tommy Boy A&R was dropping two hundred dollars on a bottle of Grey Goose to get into a party.

Still, outsiders were riveted by this new scene, where Jay-Z, Damon Dash, Puffy, Leo, and the SKE kids reshaped New York nightlife, with me as their DJ. I knew I'd really made my way into the larger culture when I saw myself in a Ben Stiller script.

At the 1996 VH-1 Fashion Awards, Stiller and Drake Sather

played male models in a popular sketch satirizing the pretensions of the downtown fashion world. When Stiller set out to expand the sketch into a feature film, I got a call to play myself in the opening scene, DJing at Life.

The script went like this: I spin "Relax," by Frankie Goes to Hollywood, triggering several male models to start violently attacking people. An eastern European woman charges the booth and orders me to change the music. I respond, "Nobody tells Mark Ronson what to play!" She then grabs my wrist and snaps it in two, and I crumple to the ground, whimpering.

Stiller was a giant. That he was an Upper West Side Jew made him feel like the cool older guy who went to my Hebrew school—except generationally funny. Comedy was my next great love after music. I couldn't believe my name had passed through his brain, through his fingers, and onto the page.

I went up to his production office to meet and read for him. I only had one line—how hard could it be? I was playing myself, after all, and I'd spent enough time in comedy clubs, and hanging out with comedians, to think I had a decent sense of humor.

I gushed about *Flirting with Disaster* and his MTV show. When I read my line—"Nobody tells Mark Ronson what to play!"—it landed flatter than a factory-sealed LP. Second try, still lifeless. I added a whimper as I crumpled that only made it worse.

I made it into *Zoolander* anyway—just without any lines. Turns out DJs have rhythm, comics have timing, and they're not as interchangeable as I'd thought.

THIRTEEN

I N 1999, THE PREDICTED Y2K bug had people panic-buying batteries, bottled water, and SpaghettiOs. But I was too busy working to worry. The nineties were ending. After six years climbing the club circuit, at twenty-three, I'd surpassed anything I'd imagined for myself as a DJ. Club gigs were on fire. I'd landed the *New York Times* Sunday Styles cover for a piece called "Deejays Make the World Go Round." A lady from *New York* magazine called to say they wanted me on their cover. Gigs were pouring in so fast that I was passing extras to friends like Oprah handing out cars—everyone was eating.

I was so omnipresent that the press made up a new term for it, "celebrity DJ." Whether it was because I played music for famous people or my ubiquity made *me* into a minor celebrity, the label made me wince. But this was, of course, where my ambition had taken me. I had connections, cultural cachet, and influence. I wasn't complaining. But there was another side of me, too—the person who had grinded for years gaining credibility in the underground scene. Back then, the highest dream would have been seeing my name on a flyer for a Bill and Carlos party—to be downtown famous. Stars of a subculture, not *the* culture. The microcelebrities of New York hadn't yet been vaulted to the national stage. And yet, after the blur of two thousand nights, I looked up and things were different.

At this point, my range of gigs was absurd, bordering on surreal. One night, I wrapped an office party uptown for Martha Stewart, sped to Flatiron for Rawkus Records' *Soundbombing II* release party— my set sandwiched between Pharoahe Monch and Mos Def—and then capped the night in the East Village at my regular club gig. Like Arnold in *The Terminator*, I'd walk into each room and scan the crowd, calculating taste, risk, and kill potential. Every room was to be destroyed.

Then, one afternoon in March 1999, I got a glimpse of a higher rung of DJing—and suddenly my reign at the top felt wobbly. Mighty Mi and I were in the living room of DJ AM's Hollywood apartment. His turntables faced the TV, the screen paused on a frame from some DJ battle, the lanky combatant frozen in time. Each of AM's turntables held a copy of Run-DMC's "Here We Go (Live at the Funhouse)" marked up with stickers. AM stepped behind the decks, cued up Run's verse, and let it rock:

> *Rhymes so def, rhymes galore*
> *Rhymes that you never even heard before*
> *Now if you say you heard my rhyme, then we gonna have to fight*
> *'Cause I just made the motherfuckers up last night*

He repeated the line *'Cause I just made the motherfuckers up last night*, going back and forth between the two records. His hands accelerated as the phrase shortened to "Just made the mother." Then his movements became a blur, his fingertips whizzing from the vinyl to the fader and back, pausing, rewinding, muting—until he *altered the sequence* of Run's words to say, *Just…fucked…yo…mother… last…night.*

He ran the foul-mouthed phrase a few more times before punching stop on both Technics.

It was the most mind-blowing display of dexterity I'd ever seen.

"Dude. How'd you learn that shit??!!" I asked, still trying to process.

"Man…just been in the crib watching old DMC battles and teaching myself the routines. Crazy what you can do when you quit smoking crack." He gave a gallows chuckle and took a drag of his cigarette.

Looking at the scattered VHS tapes and overflowing ashtrays, I said, "I guess it helps you haven't left this room in a year," half joking, half in awe. Not long ago, we were peers. Watching him push himself to such mastery in so little time was remarkable. He'd always been a great party DJ, but now he was on the verge of something extraordinary.

"You gotta come to New York and spin with me," I said, still excited. "They're gonna bug when they see you do that shit."

Back in New York, where I was still "the guy"—for now—I played every Friday in the basement of Life wedged in a corner between a road case, the back wall, and the set of stairs that led down to the VIP. Most mobile Bar Mitzvah DJs had slicker setups than this. But sometimes it's not the booth, it's the platform. And Life was still the epicenter of downtown.

Some coked-up guy in a dress shirt waved me down. "Can I get two cosmos and a double vodka soda?" I nodded, letting him fidget for ten minutes before he realized I wasn't the bar. I'm wearing headphones. He should know better.

Two hours later, with the room at its peak, I mixed EPMD into Biggie, then hit them with AC/DC into Rufus and Chaka Khan's "You Got the Love"—a curveball blast of funked-out fuzz guitar meeting Chaka's gritty mezzo-soprano. Dominique Trenier, a hip Black music executive with big brown eyes and a voice so raspy it sounded like he'd been gargling razor blades since the eighties, danced his way to the booth. His colorful silk shirt had sweat stains. He was usually one of the last on the floor.

"Yo, I got this white girl on my label with the illest voice! I don't know what her record's gonna sound like, all I know is…it's gotta feel like one of your sets. Chaka Khan, AC/DC, Biggie. All that shit!" he shouted over the music.

"Sounds good! Bring her by the crib."

A few years earlier, Dom had given me a shot at remixing Seal's "Fly Like an Eagle" for the *Space Jam* soundtrack. I was barely qualified, with just a shelved De La Soul remix to my name. Still, he spent a Saturday standing over me and my MPC in my bedroom, trying to coax out a greatness that I couldn't muster for him. But for some reason, he was giving me another shot. My track record hadn't changed much—just an R&B remix on MCA with Sauce Money (Jay-Z's occasional collaborator) and two beats for Funk Flex's Flip Squad All-Stars, thanks to Jessica Rosenblum, who was still queen of some of New York's rowdiest gatherings. But all those beats were me chasing trends, trying to reproduce the polished hip-pop of

Trackmasters or the grimy snap of Buckwild. Nothing distinctive. And how could I find my sound when I was bombarding my ears with everyone else's five nights a week? Yet Dom spotted potential I couldn't see in myself.

He brought his singer, Nikka Costa, to my new digs—a two-thousand-square-foot loft of brick and concrete on a stretch of Thirty-Fourth Street between Tenth and Eleventh. I shared it with Max LeRoy, who'd drifted back into my orbit. The neighborhood, caught between Hell's Kitchen and the river, had no name or vibe. But I enjoyed its nighttime silence.

Nikka and I connected instantly over Chaka, Stevie, and Zeppelin. Her father, Don Costa, was a renowned producer who'd arranged "My Way" for Sinatra. Singing on his records had made her a child star in Europe.

Soon we were getting together daily. Her husband, Justin, a celebrated Australian producer a decade older, joined us in my home studio—a spare bedroom stuffed with turntables, an MPC3000, a vintage Wurlitzer electric piano, a Korg Triton synthesizer, two digital eight-track recorders, a few guitars, and a sixteen-track Mackie mixing desk. Justin played bass, Nikka hammered away on the electric piano, and I chopped drum breaks the way I'd learned from watching Mighty Mi.

Nikka's voice was incredible, channeling Chaka, Janis, and Minnie. She'd spent a decade in Australia singing blues and Faces covers. But hip-hop was new territory. Quantized swing and crusty, jagged loops didn't move her like they moved me.

We clashed when she thought my MPC drums felt too programmed. I played her Premier's "Nas Is Like" to demonstrate how sampled beats could hit as hard and feel as nuanced as live drums. For me, blending her raw, soulful voice with those beats felt revolutionary. She wasn't convinced. It was frustrating at times, but her talent was too extraordinary not to keep trying to make it work.

Songs began to take shape, and Dom dropped in weekly to hear our demos—Nikka's growling vocals layered over Justin's Zeppelin-esque guitars and my obscure acid-jazz drum breaks. He'd bounce around the room, his excitement building with each visit, proud of the musical family he'd brought to life. Or rather from Life.

Midway through the summer, a few friends and I went to see Lauryn Hill at the Jones Beach Theater, which, on the right summer night, might be the world's greatest place to see a show. A calm breeze bounced off the South Shore as Lauryn took the stage with an eight-piece band, three backup singers, and a DJ. Songs like "Ex-Factor" and "Doo-Wop (That Thing)," from her solo masterpiece, *Miseducation*, already sounded like classics.

Her band brought muscularity without losing the dusty, rugged intricacies of the samples and breakbeats that made those recordings so beloved. Her DJ, Supreme, launched into a fierce scratch routine, cutting up the Kool Herc favorite, Herman Kelly's "Dance to the Drummer's Beat," until the whole band joined in. My brain imploded—DJ and live band as one, encapsulating my ideal sonic universe.

While Nikka and Justin summered in Australia, I got tight with John Forté, the dreadlocked producer who was close with Lauryn, having coproduced several songs on *The Score*. He guided my production, teaching me to trust my natural timing rather than letting the MPC's digital brain correct every beat.

John had grown up in Brownsville—one of Brooklyn's most crime- and poverty-ridden areas—before scoring a full scholarship to the elite prep school Exeter and, after, NYU. He was a study in contrasts: an erudite intellectual who draped himself in a hundred grand worth of diamonds most days.

One day, I was hypnotized by one of his dazzling bracelets, and he insisted I try it on. "That looks dope on you! We should go up to Jacob," he said. Jacob Arabo—aka Jacob the Jeweler—was the go-to guy for all the big-name rappers.

"Really? How much?" I asked, looking down at my wrist.

"Maybe forty grand."

Eesh. I was making good money, but I rarely saved any of it. *Maybe they'd have a smaller one?*

We cabbed it to midtown and hopped out in front of a busted-up neon sign that said 47TH STREET DIMOND EXCHANGE. As we walked in, Jay-Z was walking out and flashed us a smile. My adrenaline rush from the Hov sighting destroyed any remaining impulse control—I was ready to buy some diamonds.

When I asked for something affordable, Jacob pulled out a slender band with tiny diamonds.

"Twenty grand," he said flatly.

"Do you do layaway?"

"Layaway?" He balked. "How can I know you'll pay?"

I scrambled to think of who might vouch for me and landed on Andre Harrell—the former Uptown Records head who'd signed Heavy D, Jodeci, and Mary J. Blige. Born in the Bronx to a factory foreman and nurse's aide, he was the scene's most cultured figure. He also believed everyone should look their flyest at all times. He once told me I was doing too well to still be running around in Lacoste polos and blue jeans and took me to a Versace boutique. I bought a gorgeous blue-gray blazer with Edo-like waves stitched into the fabric. Andre taught me clothes could be art.

Jacob returned from making the call.

"Okay. How much do you have?"

"Five grand," I said, clumsily pulling a wad of bills from my pocket.

I'd saved ten thousand in cash from a year of gigs, plus another five grand in my Bank Leumi account. How I'd cover the rent was tomorrow's problem. My only current concern was leaving with the bracelet today.

The queasy knot in my stomach as I handed over the cash was immediately countered by the dopamine rush of this unhinged impulse buy. I stepped onto Seventh Avenue with a spring in my step and the equivalent of a Nissan Maxima strapped on my wrist.

That night, I was DJing at Shine, a club perched in the shell of the old New Music Café. A reinvention like this was par for the course in nightlife's Whac-A-Mole world. A club runs hot until someone shoots up the place—or worse, the D-listers swarm in. Then it's curtains. A new owner slaps on a fresh coat of paint, rechristens it, and reopens the doors. In New York, clubs don't die; they just change names.

Wednesdays at Shine was Home Cookin', a Bill Spector party imported from Miami, where DJs played outdoors and barbecue was served. But this was New York, so we played indoors and brought in spaghetti from Pepe Rosso down the street.

The turntables were onstage, which I hated. Put me in a corner with a clear view of the dance floor—blissfully unnoticed—and I'm happy. Here, I was front and center. Suddenly, I was self-conscious and hyperaware of every little thing I did. At one point, an overhead light caught my new bracelet sending prisms of light refracting around the room like a disco ball. I suddenly felt ridiculous.

On my friend John, a bracelet like this read like a rags-to-riches story. On me, not so much. The diamonds made me look like some clown cruising South Beach in a banana-yellow Porsche 911 blasting "Damn It Feels Good to Be a Gangsta."

The next day, I went back to Jacob alone and politely asked for my five grand back.

"I don't give refunds," he said. Jesus. *Why had I been so impulsive?* Now I was fucked. I wracked my brain to think of *anything* that I could pull off from this blinding palace of bling.

"What about a Magen David?" I asked, playing the Jew card.

"I could make you that," he said, his tone warmer.

Two weeks later, I returned to pick it up. Standing in front of the mirror, I fastened the thin silver clasp behind my neck. It was over the top, but as the six gleaming points settled against my collarbone, the weight of heritage felt unexpectedly right.

* * *

Nikka and Justin returned to New York, and armed with six strong demos, we headed into Electric Lady Studios to record. I turned off West Eighth Street and walked through the front door and down a short staircase, treading on worn purple carpet that had to be older than me. A black cat darted past and scowled.

"Don't mind Jimi," a voice said. "Hi, I'm Mary, the studio manager."

"Hi…Mark. I'm looking for Studio A," I replied.

Mary led me through two sets of heavy wooden doors into a rectangular room that looked like the cockpit of a seventies TV spaceship. A massive blue mixing desk, covered in an endless array of knobs, lights, faders, and meters, spanned the width. Each wall was lined with racks stuffed with gear—more knobs, buttons, and meters. Twin hulking reel-to-reel machines loomed in the far corner. The glow and hum from a thousand electric boxes was dizzying. I'd only been here three minutes, but I never wanted to leave.

Through a huge window lay yet another vast wooden room, with a grand piano, amps, and drum kits. A strange tapestry covered the far wall—a cosmic scene featuring a three-eyed blond alien piloting a spacecraft. Mary mentioned that Hendrix, tripping on acid, had discovered the artist in a nightclub and commissioned the piece on the spot, although Jimi overdosed before it was finished.

Justin stood by a drum kit adjusting vintage microphones on towering boom stands, tilting and repositioning each by millimeters. A kid my age in black jeans and a tee steadily whacked the snare drum while Justin paced in between the live room and the control room, making tiny adjustments. Engrossed, Justin barely nodded hello—this was clearly his happiest place. Assistants buzzed about purposefully, plugging mic cables into wall units and adjusting headphones boxes.

Soon, Questlove, the drummer for the Roots, arrived with bassist Pino Palladino and keyboardist James Poyser. Thanks to Dom's managing D'Angelo, we had D's elite band. Questlove was already a revered figure among the heads. No DJ could believe how Quest could replicate the programmed swing of Q-Tip and J Dilla—that slightly off, machine-made groove that no human drummer was supposed to achieve.

Watching Justin's command of EQs, preamps, compressors, and mics, I felt useless. I could program an MPC in my sleep, but in this analog palace, I was lost. I sat quietly in the corner, chiming in when a take was great, but I felt like the triangle player in a symphony— necessary but hardly central.

Nikka and Justin came alive at the mixing desk as the musicians brought her songs to life. It was brilliant, but also organic and acoustic sounding. I suddenly worried their goal was to replace the grit and rawness of my loops and samples with this natural sound. What I wanted was to channel the raw alchemy Lauryn Hill had unleashed that night at Jones Beach.

The second day, Questlove ducked out to Disc-O-Rama and came back with Fiona Apple's new CD, *When the Pawn...* The opening song's assault of drums, syncopated piano, and her furious vocal shocked us silent. The drums were as heavy as hip-hop, the instrumentation as dense as the Beatles'. By the end, keyboards, tape loops, strings, and plenty of noises I couldn't discern erupted into a mind-melting carnival of sound.

We'd barely recorded a hi-hat, and we'd just been knocked over by a masterpiece. We filed out in dead silence.

The week improved, though. Questlove and Pino transformed our demos with their telekinetic mastery of rhythm. Roaming Electric Lady's halls at night was like walking through a neo-soul wonderland. I passed Common—the beloved Chicago emcee whose "Resurrection" was a favorite—in the hallway, his bucket hat pulled low, a forty-ounce in hand. Erykah Badu glided between rooms with the poise of a priestess. Mary told me the studio had hit a rough patch but D'Angelo's recent stint had sparked a renaissance. She also shared wild stories about Mick, my stepfather, who'd recorded there in the eighties. She remembered him staying up for days on end, driven by perfectionism and cocaine. When he finally finished the album—*Foreigner 4*—he insisted an armored van and armed guards transport the tapes to Atlantic Records, convinced someone would rob him of his opus. The paranoid rock star god of Studio A was a far cry from the Mick I now knew. I couldn't help but marvel at this cocaine-fueled productivity. The same substance would have sent me spiraling into a panic attack and fleeing for home by 2:00 a.m. on the first night.

One evening during recording, Dom took me to Nobu, a glitzy sushi restaurant in Tribeca. A few tables over, I spotted Robin Williams. My mind raced back to my earliest childhood memory of him tucking me in. Had I imagined it? Would he even remember, given how high he'd probably been? Nerves got the better of me and I stayed put. But a little later, he rose from his table and walked toward us. As he neared, I took my shot. "Excuse me, Mr. Williams—"

He stopped.

"I have no idea if you'll remember this, but my earliest childhood memory is of you coming into my bedroom in London, at my parents' house, to tuck me in."

He paused. For a while.

"Wait, was it the house on Circus Road?"

"Yes! Yes, it was!" I couldn't believe it.

"Your parents threw some wild parties, man..."

He gave a polite nod. "Now, if you'll excuse me..."

After a few more days at the studio, we wrapped.

* * *

I left Electric Lady feeling like a musical third wheel. Maybe Nikka and Justin had worked with me just to humor Dom? Still, I flew to LA to finish the album, determined to see it through.

One morning, while I was pounding away on my MPC, Nikka walked in and tossed me a sixties prog-rock record she'd picked up at a thrift store. I threw it on, skimming around until a string of notes caught my ear. I chopped them up and programmed some hard-hitting drums à la DJ Premier. Meanwhile, Nikka was thrashing at her acoustic guitar like a redheaded Pete Townshend live at Leeds, working on another tune. Our two ideas were stylistically chalk and cheese. But then she sang a short falsetto melody that jumped out. I quickly tuned my samples to match her voice and handed her the headphones.

She paused, not seeing how the beat and her song were connected, but then she sang the first few lines. Even through the headphones, we felt the magic. We cranked it through the speakers, and Justin came in, swept up in the excitement. He added a slinky phaser bass. Nikka laid down her wild, soulful vocal and added handclaps. I thought some fuzzed-out guitar might work, so Justin overdrove the desk's recording inputs like the Beatles did on "Revolution," and I double-tracked a lead line. It was unlike anything we'd ever created before.

Dom came by later and listened, beaming. At long last, we'd made good on his vision—this imagined fusion of funk, soul, hip-hop, and rock 'n' roll he'd envisioned one sweaty night at Life.

"What's it called?" he asked.

Nikka answered, " 'Like a Feather.' "

"Really?" He shrugged, underwhelmed by the name, then leaned forward with a grin. "Again!"

* * *

For those who work nights, taking New Year's Eve off is unthinkable. It's the one night you can charge five or ten times your normal rate. The idea of clocking out or casually sipping champagne with friends was as realistic as Santa's elves filing for December PTO.

I started the night at MTV's Times Square studio, DJing on camera in between Carson Daly's intros for Sugar Ray, Bush, and Blink-182. Next, I fought my way through thousands of pedestrians and partygoers to get up to 254 West Fifty-Fourth Street, where a very rich person had rented out Studio 54 to ring in the new century in the most famous nightclub of the previous one. No expense was spared, and not much taste was used either. Trays of lobster adorned every table. Apparently, no one told him that at the real Studio 54, people were too high or too busy fucking to eat.

I brought my boy Lord Sear—an underground DJ and rapper from Uptown with a great mic voice—to hype up the crowd. He was so excited by all the celebs, he came off more like an announcer on *The Price Is Right*: "Yo, we got David Lee Roth in the house!" Diamond Dave didn't seem to mind. Harvey Keitel was less pleased.

As midnight approached, I played my trusty copy of "Le Freak" with the Black Passions logo, an ironic contribution to our Y2K apocalypse jitters. Plus, the song was inspired by this very building after Chic's Nile Rodgers and Bernard Edwards were once rejected at the door of Studio 54 (their original hook: "Aaaaaaah, fuck off!"). At 11:59:50, Sear led the countdown, I dropped Snoop and Dre's "The Next Episode," and for better or worse, the world didn't shut down. Grace Jones stormed the stage at 4:00 a.m., in a nod to the original Studio 54, and to remind us New York was cooler, weirder, and more glamorous before our time.

The party showed no signs of ending, so I took out a plastic baggie and crouched behind my tables, then raised a bump of blow to my nose in homage to the original 54. This night was barreling into the morning. Resolutions could wait.

* * *

People were losing their shit over "Like a Feather." Virgin Records saw dollar signs, Tommy Hilfiger wanted it to soundtrack his next commercial, and Chris Rock booked Nikka to perform it on the series finale of his late-night HBO show after hearing only sixty seconds. But far more important than all of that, I'd finally produced a record I was proud of. Proud enough to play in the club even, so I went up to Sterling Sound to have it pressed onto my own acetate. The studio engineer hunched over a lathe—a bulky device resembling an industrial sewing machine, with a twelve-inch platter at its base. After listening once and tweaking some dials, he placed a pristine, smooth piece of vinyl on the platter and pressed play on my digital audio tape, and the machine's head descended onto the blank vinyl. Slowly, it began carving into the surface, writing our song into the wax.

Technically, the stylus was etching grooves by drawing amplitudes and frequencies. But from where I stood, this machine was sculpting music.

The purpose of an acetate is to create a sonically perfect master copy, which is then electroplated and turned into a "stamp" to press the audio onto more vinyl, which gets slipped into sleeves and shipped to stores. Watching the lathe do its thing, my mind drifted to the engineer who performed this task for "Le Freak," producing a master disc that would go on to birth millions of replicas. And how, one day in 1978, a DJ like Black Passions Inc. walked into Sounds, bought his copy, and spread its magic across nightclubs, block parties, cookouts, and roller rinks throughout the city. Then, in 1994, I bought his old copy off a street vendor on West Fourth Street and spun this disco classic across New York City a thousand more times. The sacred magic of "Le Freak" belonged to Chic, but its gospel was spread by DJs like us. The lathe was a mint, printing joy and ecstasy. The engineer printed up a label, slapped it on the disc, and sent me on my way.

A week later, armed with my new acetate and a customary excess of vinyl, I headed out to Centro-Fly, a brand-new dance club on West Twenty-First, to play the release party for D'Angelo's *Voodoo*. The album had taken D five years to complete. People were so ecstatic it was finally here, the evening seemed destined for music history before I dropped the first song.

Tom Sisk, the club's owner, led me to the booth, a plush, blue-carpeted den with velvet walls and blue suede banquettes, decorated nicer than most apartments. Centro-Fly hadn't officially opened, but Tom was hoping to lure superstar DJs like Sasha and Erick

Morillo with this booth as his bait. It had couches, private bars, state-of-the-art equipment, and a huge open window overlooking an adoring crowd. It was the opposite of Life, where there was nowhere to sit, nothing to drink, and I was so buried in the crowd, people assumed I was the bar or coat check. More important, Tom was trying to bring dance floors back to clubland. Bless him.

Dom and D'Angelo brought out Black royalty—Lil' Kim, Evander Holyfield, Lenny Kravitz, Erykah Badu, Veronica Webb—and five hundred of downtown's finest. I kept it soulful for the first few hours before a fun diversion into Honkytown with some eighties classics. An excited Mos Def ran into the booth and grabbed the mic, proclaiming, "YOU ARE IN THE MIDDLE OF A MARK RONSON EIGHTIES MEGAMIX…mix…mix" over the icy synths of Eurythmics' "Sweet Dreams (Are Made of This)."

When the time and tempo were right, I pulled out my virgin acetate of "Like a Feather." I was ready for the song's true test. As a DJ, the cardinal sin is clearing the dance floor, and nothing could be more humiliating than doing it with one's own record. My reputation as a DJ and my fledgling career as a producer were riding on this. As I mixed it out of D'Angelo's "Devil's Pie," I held my breath, but a mass exodus didn't happen. People were digging it.

A heavy thump sounded at the booth door. I opened it to find DJ Premier standing there, alone. *Holy shit.* I waved him in and returned to the decks, sneaking glances from the corner of my eye, beyond starstruck. One of my all-time heroes was five feet away, staring at the floor, nodding his head deeply to the track. *But why was he in here?*

"Yo, what is this?" he asked.

"It's, uh, Nikka Costa, sir." *Did I just say sir?*

"Who did the beat?" Uh-oh. He must have thought someone was biting his style. He'd come to call them out—or worse. I was in deep shit.

"I did." The jig was up.

"You did this?!"

His tone was incredulous but also...delighted?

"This shit is haaaaarrrrrrrd," he said, his features twisting into a stankface as he bobbed ferociously until the song's very last kick drum.

I remembered my childhood bedroom—me on the top bunk, loading Gang Starr's *Daily Operation* into the tape deck. That cassette sparked my deep love affair with this music, leading to thousands of nights in basements, bars, lounges, dorm rooms, and loft parties, honing an eclectic style for years until some cool dude paired me with a singer, and together we created something dope enough to rock in a DJ set. And now, the man who started it all stood in my booth like Yoda, telling me, "You did good, kid."

All I managed was "Thank you," but inwardly, I was experiencing every emotion in my DJ's journey simultaneously, my soul experiencing its own supernova.

There wasn't much time to talk, though, because a dance floor waits for no one. Even the funkiest track won't keep people dancing at 2:00 a.m. on a winter Monday if they've never heard it before.

I had to get the tempo up fast. But how exactly?

My brain mapped a route across a riverbed of Stevie Wonder tunes. I played "Maybe Your Baby" (93 BPM), a funky bridge out of "Feather." Then into "As" (103 BPM), stylistically different, but seeing as they're both Stevie, I knew the crowd would allow it. As Gerry Brown's drumming drove "As" to 107 BPM, I nudged the pitch control and mixed in "All I Do" at minus two and eased it to zero. If ever there were a song of pure, unadulterated love etched into black vinyl, this was it. "All I Do" might be labeled disco, but really, it's a song of praise. Accordingly, everyone lifted their heads and sang up to the heavens. Stevie's vocal burst through me, and for a change, I sang with the crowd. Singing, swaying, and connected with a hundred soul fanatics still out on the floor on a freezing Monday night in New York City.

These were my people.

ONE LAST SONG

This is how we chill from '93 'til...

SOULS OF MISCHIEF, "93 'TIL INFINITY" (1993)

L AST SUNDAY, I strapped my daughter, Ruthie, to my chest and headed out to cruise downtown. She's nearly two and admittedly too big for a Baby Bjorn, but we've been riding like this since she was tiny and I'm just not ready to give it up.

We pass the Thompson Street playground, where Bill Spector used to tell stories about DJ Clark Kent tearing down Mars, as we scarfed down sandwiches from Alidoro's next door. Then Union, where I bought my first Pumas with the fat red laces at sixteen, because that was what the NASA kids wore. Funny how these downtown streets, once a wild new frontier for me, are the only hood that Ruthie has ever known. As we cross Thompson Street, I spot a familiar face and feel a jolt of excitement. I know her from the club days, but I can't find a name or context. She has pale skin and an oval face, like a pretty ghost. But when we pass, she glances at me like I'm the ghost. Or maybe she's staring because I've got someone the size of an emperor penguin buckled to my chest.

This happens all the time in New York—faces trigger a vague recognition, but I can't place them. Was it someone I got high and joked around with after hours? The cashier from the club? Or just another regular I'd see, week after week, on the dance floor? I always let them pass, wondering what memories we've left on the table.

Ruthie swings her legs happily, her pink Nikes slamming into my thighs. She says something I don't quite catch.

"What was that?" I ask.

"Reh-koods," she repeats, pointing at an ad featuring a woman flipping through vinyl.

It catches me off guard, and I tear up. She often pulls the Dolly Parton *Trio* album from the shelf, hands it to me, and, when I put it on the turntable, watches mesmerized as the platter spins. I think of my own dad, a young boy in Hampstead, London, alone in a dark study, taking the Stevie Wonder single out of its sleeve and setting the needle onto the tiny groove. The electricity between him and the music. And how it passed to me. I've got a picture of me at Ruthie's age, in the living room of my parents' first flat on George Street, gripping a seven-inch in one hand, a Leon Haywood LP bigger than my head in the other.

"Reh-koods" have been life's most constant companions. Looking out at this SoHo grid, I imagine all of my former selves on the street, crisscrossing and converging, lugging crates into bars and nightclubs and house parties. Long before I was a father, I was carrying something joyous. But I haven't DJed with records in years. Instead, I use Serato, software that lets me manipulate songs on my laptop via turntables and CD players. Instead of crates, I have a MacBook. My back thanks me, but the truth is, I'm not the DJ I used to be. Back then, limited by crate space, I'd sit on my apartment floor crafting my entire set beforehand, agonizing over every choice.

Should I pack the hefty double-disc *Classic Funk Mastercuts* or the equally bulky *Classic Jazz-Funk Mastercuts?* Asking myself, will the crowd be funky or jazz-funky? Do I bring the Isley Brothers' *Go for Your Guns*, with the all-time slow jam "Footsteps in the Dark (Parts 1 & 2)," or their album *The Heat Is On*, which has "Fight the Power" *and* "For the Love of You"? Now, with Serato, I rock up to the club with the entire history of music under my arm. But the sheer number of choices is paralyzing. With seconds left on Drake and Wizkid's "One Dance," I frantically scroll through thousands of tracks and land on "Ring of Fire" by Johnny Cash purely because the computer says they're both 104 BPM. Meanwhile, these songs have as much in common as a goldfish and a lampshade.

Serato enables a boundless creativity. I think about DJ AM, who died in 2009, and imagine all the genius shit he'd be doing if he were still alive, his friends gathered around him, jaws on the floor, like the old days. He loved Serato, using it to invent routines we could only dream of. Hell, he made me a convert.

Still, I miss turning around in the booth and seeing my most cherished possessions sticking out at odd angles, each one telling a story. A cranberry juice stain on a white label from that night Mariah Carey burst into the booth, demanding Princess's "Say I'm Your Number One." Or the mildew creeping up a Players Association record, courtesy of when I flooded my apartment on Franklin Street. We hauled our treasured possessions to work each night, turning soulless closets into temples of sound and memory.

Ruthie's happiest when I'm telling stories, so I keep a running monologue while we walk. Lucky for us, downtown is one big storybook. I point to a bar on Spring Street I DJed so long ago, the name escapes me—Jet Set? Jet Lounge? "Dadda played music here when he was a boy," I tell her.

"Dadda. Music," she replies.

I wonder if Ruthie will ever get to see me DJ. It's unlikely I'll be doing this in fifteen years. I have no old footage to show her, no viral clips. Part of what made our era so special was the absence of surveillance. People were completely in the moment. The trade-off is that Ruthie will never see me when I was at my best.

Now at suppertime, we sit outside at Bar Pitti, a Village favorite I've been coming to half my life. Hejay, the waitress, has been here almost that long and makes a fuss over us. Maybe I'm projecting, but she seems pleasantly surprised I got it together in time to be a father. I think of the thousand times I stumbled in here with half a brain on a Sunday, hurriedly ordering a glass of red to fend off Saturday night's headache. Back then, I liked the hangovers. They wrapped the world in soft gauze, dulling the edges of my anxious brain.

The old fears, the old sadness—they're still there. As with everyone. But these days, I welcome them as if they're familiar guests at the table. They come, but they also go. I'm not sober, but I also don't fling myself at stimulation and chaos any chance I can get. Looking back at the early days, I can't believe what I put my body through, how normal I thought it was, and the ways in which it kept me disassociated from the real stuff of life. Ruthie goes for a knife, and I grab it just in time. The old hungover me wouldn't have stood a chance.

Once she's had her fill—and left enough sidewalk spaghetti to feed half the pigeons in the Village—we head to my mother and Mick's for our usual Sunday visit. The door opens, and Ruthie shouts, "Meeeek!" and bolts toward him on the couch. Mick was diagnosed with Parkinson's a few years ago. It was devastating. He once shredded solos that boggle my mind—my childhood guitar god, Slash, once told me he learned every one of them. Now I catch Mick staring at the acoustic in the living room, hesitant to pick it up, afraid of what might no longer be in his hands.

Mick spends a lot of the day glued to Premier League football and crime dramas, but he lights up when Ruthie is nearby. She adores him. This year, even as we've visited him in various floodlit hospital rooms that reeked of Lysol and sickness, she never shied from perching on his bed, wrapping her hand around two of his fingers while he drifted in and out of consciousness. Thankfully, there are plenty of videos of him in his Foreigner heyday. I can't wait until the day I show Ruthie what he looked like onstage, wielding his sunburst Les Paul to melt the faces of twenty thousand fans.

My mother joins us on the couch while I watch Ruthie doodling giant circles.

"I used to stare at you like that," she says. "I must've saved every drawing you did."

Her eyes mist up in a way I've never seen before. Back when we were kids, she was carrying such weight—her pain, the divorce, Mick losing everything, and worrying about me during my messiest years, when I looked ashen and gray. I can't tell if she's emotional because she's remembering what it was like to look at me at Ruthie's age, because she still loves me with the same intensity, or simply because she's happy to see me at peace now. I'll gladly take any of the three.

Finally, Ruthie and I head home. Grace, my wife, is away. The house feels too quiet without her. I tap-dance my best to distract Ruthie (and myself) from how much we miss her. The force of Grace's love and the calm she's brought to my life are so unwavering that they ground me even in her absence. She has a beautiful voice, made for lullabies, and if she were here, she would be serenading Ruthie at bedtime. Tonight, Ruthie settles for my off-key falsetto rendition of Neil Young's "Comes a Time." She lies heavy on my chest, echoing the end of each line. When her voice is faint enough, I know I'm safe to lower her into the crib.

I'm extra careful these days, still healing from two torn tendons—courtesy of trying to turn a hundred-pound floor monitor to face the crowd at an overseas gig—because the venue's PA system was shit. For a career that doesn't exactly scream stuntman-level danger, I've accumulated quite a toll: the bog-standard tinnitus, a destroyed SI joint, chronic neck issues from decades of asymmetrical posture, and synovitis in my right metatarsal from twenty-five years of tapping tempo. Or, as I like to call it, DJ Foot.

I close the door, and peaceful parental energy gives way to the buzzy anticipation of a rare night out. Tonight, leaving Ruthie with the sitter, I'm off to Tiki Disco to see my boys DJ Eli Escobar and Lloyd spin. It's been far too long since I've heard some brilliant DJs, and I need it—for my soul and a dose of inspiration.

The party is at the Knockdown Center, a repurposed factory in an industrial stretch of Queens called Maspeth. These days, it's funny how few parties happen in Manhattan. During the nineties, Brooklyn supplied a huge chunk of Manhattan's nightlife crowd, but it was rarely where we went to work. Now, with Manhattan too expensive to live in for most young people, clubland has migrated to Brooklyn. It didn't come as a surprise, but when I first heard people were partying out in Ridgewood, Queens, about ten years ago, it made me realize just how out of the loop I'd become.

Eli meets me at the side door, because the front is mobbed and I no longer know every door girl and bouncer in the five boroughs. We weave through an underground maze, and slip through a back door and into the outdoor DJ booth, where I'm greeted by the night air and monitors blasting. I've never been here before, and it's revelatory. The booth alone is its own mini-party, with twenty faces lit up, dancing around Lloyd, who's locked into a bouncy electro joint. Glazed with perma-grins, I can't tell if they're high on Ecstasy or just vibing heavy. Either way, in no time, I'm smiling and bouncing, too.

I look out into the crowd and then it really hits me—two thousand people in various states of dance bliss fill the outdoor space of this defunct industrial yard. Hundreds more are grooving in the windows of the surrounding buildings. It's like a street carnival— but more than that. They're facing the booth. Not because of some EDM spectacle with LED screens and pyrotechnics blitzing their attention, but because Eli and Lloyd are two low-key heroes who've spent decades mastering their craft and are now sharing sounds cultivated through decades of musical reverence, and receiving waves of this crowd's love in return.

I forgot how I miss this.

Lloyd finishes and passes the headphones to Eli, who spins the jog wheel on the CDJ with manic focus, hunting for the perfect opening. He bobs enthusiastically to Lloyd's last track, but I recognize that "bob"—it's nerves. No matter how many times you've done it, those final moments before playing your first song always feel like standing at the edge of a cliff. He opens with DJ Dai's "Duke," and the crowd loses it.

Eli's one of New York's finest dance music DJs. Even though he cut his teeth as a hip-hop DJ, working many of the same spots I did in the nineties, his heart was in house music and soaring eighties synth-pop à la Talk Talk. When New York's gate-kept dance-club DJing scene proved impenetrable, he spent the next decade grinding in downtown bottle-service clubs that tested every ounce of his love for music. His release came playing in unpretentious spaces like (Sub)-Mercer—a two-hundred-cap basement under the Mercer Hotel that became a refuge for dancers tired of endless swanky lounges.

Tiki Disco started small—just a few hundred people—but he and Lloyd kept at it for a decade. Then, as New York emerged from the pandemic, a new generation discovered the clubs. These kids wanted nothing to do with the money and status obsession that had dominated the city's nightlife for twenty years. They wanted to dance again. Hundreds, then thousands began flocking to Tiki and Eli's other gigs. Now in his late forties, he's become a nightlife icon. A girl in the crowd waves a sign that says ELI, WILL YOU MARRY ME?

Watching them tonight, I feel the weight of what I've been missing. This is the magic of a residency—a crowd that trusts you like family, letting you take them anywhere. That trust lets Eli and Lloyd play fearlessly, weaving Riva Starr, Donna Summer, and Underworld into a seamless patchwork. Each selection is so good, I keep double-checking my Auto-Shazam is on.

A twenty-something blond girl in sunglasses compliments my Deee-Lite T-shirt and asks what I'm doing here.

"I've known Eli and Lloyd for decades," I tell her. "We came up DJing together."

"Oh, you used to DJ? That's cool!" she says.

After chatting a bit more, she pauses.

"Wait, are you Mark Ronson?"

"That's right."

"'Valerie' is one of my favorite songs of all time," she says, smiling. I thank her. And it's true, these days, I'm more known for making records than playing them. After the Nikka Costa record, I started building a career creating my own music. That's when DJing changed for me. I was writing and producing massive hits: "Valerie," "Uptown Funk," "Electricity," "Nothing Breaks Like a Heart." It wasn't all pop—and my joy and pain ran through it all. But each of these tracks was made for people to dance to. And when people came out to see me DJ, they expected to hear these songs. In the nineties, I'd catch veteran DJs playing three-month-old tracks and think, *Wow, nobody's told him.* Now I've become that person—except I'm spinning my fifteen-year-old hits.

I love dropping "Uptown Funk" and seeing the happiness it brings. I'm as proud of it as anything I've ever had a hand in. But if I hadn't helped create it, I doubt I'd be playing it in every set. It's a banger but also, at this point, a wedding tune, too. I read somewhere that brides now ban it from the groom's playlist, dreading the inevitable best-man choreo.

What fascinates me is how much more excited people get when I spin it, as opposed to any other DJ. Sadly, it's not like Bruno Mars is going to magically spring from my laptop. But I also get it: People enjoy music more when they're dancing in front of the person who made it. And don't get me wrong, I'm *beyond* grateful for all of it. But it's a weird thing that's happened to DJing. Most of the Vegas headliners aren't DJs; they're producers who've made giant hits. People show up to see them press play on those songs. What Eli and Lloyd are doing tonight, though—that's pure DJing.

Many of my friends from the old days, like Lloyd and Eli, are still going strong. But many are gone forever—promoters who gave me my first gigs, bouncers who helped me load my crates into cabs at the end of the night, and the dancers I looked forward to seeing every week.

DJ Jules is in Los Angeles, working as the creative curator at Joopiter—a Sotheby's for the hip-hop generation. He tracks down pieces that deserve to be treated as cultural artifacts, like Slick Rick's exquisite jewelry—those oversized chains from his album covers—and turns them into curated exhibits and high-profile auctions.

Mighty Mi was one of the first New York club DJs to head to Vegas. He traded the unpredictability of gigging here for the steady paycheck of a big nightclub residency, opening for massive EDM acts who couldn't hold a candle to his skills. He still hasn't stopped making underground heat on his MPC, releasing records with legends like Ghostface Killah and Big Daddy Kane.

A few have stayed. DJ Belinda is still DJing and scouring the internet for soulful tracks—from Brooklyn to Seoul to South Africa—to lift her crowd. She knows the nineties might have been the best era of clubbing, but her love for DJing and discovery keeps her moving forward. Like all of us who've been at it this long, she goes through phases of hating everything in her crate. But she always comes back.

Lloyd comes over, and I can barely make out every third word he says over "Kilo," by the Martinez Brothers. I laugh anyway. He has a rogue's talent for saying the unsayable and getting away with it.

Whenever I see Lloyd, I'm painfully reminded of our mutual friend Blu Jemz, who died six years ago from cancer. When I moved out of DJing and into making records, Blu Jemz was the one who kept me tethered to the clubs and, in turn, to my love for DJing. All the best parties I ever played in New York, post–Sweet Thang, were places Jemz dragged me to. For years we did a Friday night show on East Village Radio, broadcasting right from First Avenue and First Street. On summer nights we'd prop the glass doors open and turn it into a block party, Jemz slightly tipsy, caustically narrating the scene outside to our listeners at home.

Our last job together was supposed to be a gig he got us at House of Yes. By the time the date rolled around, he was too sick to play. I went on alone, but the booth felt emptier than it ever had. Since he's been gone, I often feel like I don't have any link to nighttime in New York at all.

On the Uber ride back to Manhattan, I ask the driver to tune to the throwback station. Fatman Scoop's "Be Faithful" comes on. After leaving his promotion job at Tommy Boy, Scoop recorded a string of anthems that moved crowds from LA to Tokyo. He died last year at fifty-six, onstage performing them, still moving the crowd.

The cadence of loss has become painfully frequent in the DJ world. Many have left us decades too soon: Clark Kent, DJ Neva, Mister Cee, Manny Ames, Paul Nice. Many of them were still at the top of their game right until the end.

The driver, Abul, takes Canal Street and we pass the old New Music Café. There it was—the party where I made my name, where I first found my own musical family, the people who, every Tuesday night, trusted me to lead them somewhere higher. Nearly three decades have passed, but I still feel that charge of pulling up and seeing the line snaking around West Broadway, all of us so excited for the night ahead. As we pull away onto Sixth Avenue, I swear I see their shadows still imprinted on the sidewalk.

* * *

A few nights later, I'm spinning at a fashion week party in DUMBO. A lot of money has gone into dressing up the raw industrial space tonight—warm, red lighting, oversized floral centerpieces, and rich drapery lining the walls. The crowd is chic, a good-looking mix of New Yorkers who wouldn't have felt out of place at a Bill and Carlos party thirty years ago. Someone gets up to make a toast and then introduces me. I know what's coming. I start playing, and people take their phones out, filming me, as I try hard to give them something to film besides a guy standing still, pressing illuminated buttons.

There's more documenting than partying. I'm going through the motions, too: "Uptown Funk" into "Valerie" into "Dance the Night" from *Barbie*. Then I look up for a moment and catch a guy dancing. His movements seem performative, the checked-out body language of someone calculating their exit strategy. This isn't how any of these people would move at a bar, or a rave, or a club, on a night that they chose to go out, for a DJ they genuinely wanted to see. After a few more obligatory songs, they'll have fulfilled their social contract and head home. In an instant, I feel an old determination welling up inside of me. I refuse to settle for this auto-pilot mode that the crowd and I have set ourselves to.

I remember the old me, walking into clubs with no hits of my own, just crates of music and an instinct for reading the room. I flash back to Sunday, to Eli and Lloyd's set, too. Something snaps into place. I pull out one of my old Snoop and Dre routines, cycling through four bars of West Coast classics, and start to build momentum. On "Nuthin' but a G Thang," I drop the volume and let them sing "baaaaby" before surprising them with "Gin & Juice," followed by a swift wordplay transition into Nas's "Oochie Wally" right on the "six in the morning" lyric. For one breathless moment, time freezes as they process what just happened and they start to come alive.

I dig deeper, pulling out tracks I haven't played in years—Donna Summer, Stardust, Sylvester—and new ones I haven't been brave enough to try.

The energy changes. Everyone stops watching me and turns inward, to each other. Phones are put away. It now looks like a real dance floor. We could be back at New Music Café. The temperature goes up five degrees. I'm earning this crowd the old way.

A few more songs in, the room is throbbing and the crowd is at a precipice. Digging through my crates, I find it—like a needle in a haystack—the perfect record. It's exactly what I need to crack the room open—to give people a reason to be alive.

My pulse quickens as I cue it up. *This* song—like a gift I can't wait to give, the kind where you can barely contain your excitement knowing it's exactly what they need but don't know they want.

In the headphones, I bring it back and give it a *jhugga-jhugga*.

It's time. I count it in—

One.

Two.

Three.

And the beat drops.

ACKNOWLEDGMENTS

The idea to write this book first came to me on January 8, 2022. That night, the owners of Le Bain were throwing a birthday celebration for James, aka Blu Jemz, one of my closest friends for twenty-five years. He'd passed away a few years earlier, but Le Bain had been his second home, and despite his absence, he was always the life of the party, so commemorating his birthday felt necessary. His dear friend and DJ partner, Eli Escobar, invited me to play that night.

Earlier that day, surrounded by my records, I kept thinking about James. I noticed the kelly green spine of a record I hadn't pulled out in twenty years. I knew exactly what it was—*Trends of Culture*, an indie hip-hop record—and even the color of the sleeve took me right back to standing at the counter of Rock and Soul in 1993, handing over my five dollars to buy it.

I thought about how all these records were linked to people, places, and clubs that were so important to me. Because of the inevitable erosion of time and excess, these memories were starting to fade from my mind. Far more tragic, so were some of the people who made that time in my life so electric. I realized right then that I wanted to commit these memories and experiences to the page before any more of it slipped away.

My good friend David Kuhn had been suggesting I write a book for years, but nothing had compelled me to do so until that moment.

I called and told him I wanted to chronicle my early years in the club scene, capturing the life of a working DJ during a vanished era of New York nightlife.

With the advice of David and Nate Muscato, I decided to structure the narrative around specific club nights. I began interviewing friends, fellow DJs, and clubgoers from the era to fill in that outline, which I presented to Colin Dickerman. His wry wit, intelligence, and willingness to take a chance on the Mark Ronson book nobody asked for (what, no Amy?!) told me I wanted to work with him.

What followed was a deep dive into my own experiences and the broader scene. I interviewed hundreds of DJs, promoters, dancers, doormen, bouncers, record company promo guys, and the people who ran the record stores. While crafting a memoir rather than an oral history, I still wanted to evoke as much of this world as possible. I realized there was something deeper than just the music pulling us all together—that invisible bond connecting all night people. I'm beyond grateful to everyone who contributed their memories and perspectives; there are too many to name in this short section and I'm terrified of forgetting someone. But I will find another way to recognize everybody for the sharing of these stories, anecdotes, and experiences from our glorious and misspent youth.

Thank you to David, without whom I never would have thought to write *anything* (yes, blame him). And for his early confidence in my writing, which drove me to do it myself. Thank you to Colin, who spent three years on this book with me—the first of which I was sending utter garbage. He helped me find my prose through both his superb critiques and his strategic silences (when I submitted something terrible, his lack of comment spoke volumes). More than just polishing prose and providing a pretty fucking great joke here and there, he truly understood the intersection of music, youth, discovery, and connection I was trying to capture. His edits consistently steered toward amplifying those elements while helping me discover my voice and pacing. Passages I thought would be boring to most—like my descriptions of discovering the original samples behind beloved hip-hop tracks, or the ABCs of building a room's energy—he pushed me to develop further, recognizing those were the things that might make this book unique. Plus, he responded to all my neurotic weekend texts.

Thank you to Zennor Compton at Penguin. I thought of you often while writing this and always attempted to keep my UK soul and roots within this very New York story. You also reminded me to highlight the many women who made this scene what it was. And to Venetia Butterfield, who, during a five-minute coffee (our only meeting), made a couple of brilliant off-the-cuff comments that planted the word "connection" into my brain throughout.

To my mother, Ann, and father, Laurence, well, for life itself—but specifically here, for their generosity in sharing their pasts and allowing my interpretation of shared history; to my stepmother, Michelle, and stepfather, Mick; and to my beloved siblings—Charlotte, Samantha, Alexander, Annabelle, Henrietta, David, Joshua, and stepbrothers Roman and Christopher: The family history belongs to all of us.

I'm indebted to Abe Streep, who read this book when I thought it was finished and informed me that it wasn't, urging me to address race, class, and family in a braver way—and to do a word search for "cool" (which I had apparently used seventy-three times). And for introducing me to Hannah Wilentz, who spent the last few months refining the final manuscript with me, subjecting me to an eighteen-hour-day writing boot camp. Her insights and intelligence enhanced every aspect of this book, linking personal narrative to cultural context while curing me of an unhealthy addiction to mixed metaphors and other bad habits. And also providing a few insanely good jokes.

For their early readings and insights, I thank Seb Chew, Harley Wertheimer, Richard Russell, Rightor Doyle, Isabella Massanet, Brandon Creed—my most steadfast confidant—and Caius Pawson, who, after reading, told me I needed to go back to playing vinyl again. (He was right, it's been life-changing.) To Eli and Lloyd for letting me use "Night People"—the name of their record label with James. And Rodrigo Corral, for a cover that might be too good for this book.

To all the DJs, the Night People, and to New York City itself—thank you.

And above all, to Grace, who was there for me in every way while this book consumed me unlike any other project. I hope someday Ruthie and Rosie will read these pages and not be completely embarrassed. I only ever want to make you proud. If only I were a talented enough writer to put into words how much I love you.

CREDITS

v.   Mos Def, "Climb": Thomas Joseph Dunn, Weldon Jonathan Irvine, Dante T. Smith, "Climb." *Black on Both Sides.* Rawcus, 1999.

vii.   A Tribe Called Quest, "Midnight": Kamaal Ibn John Fareed, Ali Shaheed Jones-Muhammad, Malik Izaak Taylor, "Midnight." *Midnight Marauders.* Jive, 1993.

40–41. Cypress Hill, "How I Could Just Kill a Man": Louis M. Freese, Lowell Fulsom, Jimmy McCracklin, Larry E Muggerud, Senen Reyes, "How I Could Just Kill a Man." *Cypress Hill.* Ruffhouse/Columbia, 1991.

41.   Redman, "Time 4 Sum Aksion": George Clinton, William Earl Collins, Louis M. Freeze, Lowell Fulsom, Gregory E. Jacobs, Jimmy McCracklin, Walter Morrison, Larry E. Muggerud, Reggie Noble, Senen Reyes, Larry Troutman, Roger Troutman. "Time 4 Sum Aksion" *Whut? Thee Album.* Rush Associated Labels, 1992.

70.   Gang Starr and Nice & Smooth, "DWYCK": Darryl Otis Barnes, Keith Elam, Christopher Martin, Gregory Mays, "DWYCK." *Hard to Earn.* Chrysalis/EMI, 1992.

104.   Ol' Dirty Bastard, "Brooklyn Zoo": Derrick R. L Harris, Russell T. Jones, "Brooklyn Zoo." *Return to the 36 Chambers: The Dirty Version*. Elektra, 1995.

118.   Alicia Bridges, "I Love the Nightlife": Alicia D. Bridges, Susan B. Hutcheson, "I Love the Nightlife." *Alicia Bridges*. Polydor, 1978.

125.   Junior M.A.F.I.A., "Player's Anthem": Rodolfo Antonio Franklin, Harvey Fuqua, Kimberly Jones, James Lloyd, Christopher Wallace, Lottie Wiggins, "Player's Anthem." *Conspiracy*. Undeas/Big Beat/Atlantic, 1995.

142.   Brick, "Dazz": Reginald J. Hargis, Edward D. Irons, Raymond L. Ransom, "Dazz." *Good High*. Bang, 1976.

178.   Lord Tariq and Peter Gunz, "Déjà Vu (Uptown Baby)": Walter Carl Becker, Donald Jay Fagen, "Déjà Vu (Uptown Baby)." *Make It Reign*. Columbia, 1997.

193–194.   Jay-Z, "Hard Knock Life (Ghetto Anthem)": Shawn C. Carter, Martin Charnin, Mark Howard James, Charles Strouse, "Hard Knock Life (Ghetto Anthem)." *Vol. 2… Hard Knock Life*. Roc-A-Fella/Def Jam, 1998.

206–207.   Run-DMC, "Here We Go (Live at the Funhouse)": Darryl Matthews McDaniels, Joseph Ward Simmons, "Here We Go (Live at the Funhouse)." *RUN-DMC (Expanded Edition)*. Arista/Legacy, 1984.

224.   Souls of Mischief, "93 'til Infinity": Adam Carter, William Emmanuel, Opio Lindsey, Tajai Massey, Damani Thompson, "93 'til Infinity." *93 'til Infinity*. Jive, 1993.

**Lyric Reprint Clearances by Suzanne Coffman & Dina Botts,
MUSIC RIGHTZ, INC.**

SCAN FOR THE OFFICIAL *NIGHT PEOPLE* PLAYLIST